A DREAM
SHATTERED

By
Zdenko Ornig

1

Foreword

Nothing written herein is intended to discredit the BBC Corporation or their employees and associates, or any other person or persons with regards to defamation of their character. This is my recollection of events in a chronological order and it is also my statement. This is a true story. Please be aware of some strong and explicit language embodied within the text.

What happened to me can happen to anyone, to any gender, to any person of any particular faith or race.

It took me years to overcome the anger, disbelief and self-pity and finally what is left is sadness, not directed at myself but at the void that is left behind in the wake of the turbulent and volatile situations in which there were no winners.

I had a chance and many opportunities to walk away from it all but was lured back with Barbara's promises that we would reconcile and she would lay her issues to rest. We never did reconcile. I only blame myself for not wanting to see or hear the signs of events spiralling out of control. Advice given by my work colleagues and friends went unheeded until it was too late and I paid the ultimate price.

I have taken great care not to succumb to any rumours, gossip or conspiracies and have written only of the truthful sequence of events within this book.

Barbara's real name and details of her family have been withheld since it would be of no public interest and my only wish is that these events were not my reality but rather one of my bad dreams.

My many thanks to Gabbi Draper who patiently helped with the design and artwork.
My thanks to Stephen Wilson for his help editing.
Many thanks to St Albans City Council, Dr Sawyer and Dr Friedman at Parkbury House surgery.

Without all of them this book would not have beeen published.

Zdenko

Author and Publisher

© A Dream Shattered
My life within the BBC and meeting the celebrities,
the famous and the powerful.

All matter is condensed to a slow vibration

and we are all one consciousness

experiencing itself subjectively.

There is no death, life is only a dream

and we are imagination of ourselves.

1

Meeting Barbara For The First Time

It was raining heavily whilst I waited in my car outside the BBC studios in Wood Lane, West London. My passenger was late, meaning that I would probably be late for my next journey booked by the BBC booking agency.

It was a very busy day with all the preparations for Princess Diana's funeral and we drivers were asked to do as many hours as possible. On that emotional day I spent most of the afternoon with Lord John. We went from Kensington Gardens to the Houses of Parliament, then on to BBC Bush House and Regent Street's recording studio, then on to Millbank and a few more addresses.

There were German, Italian and American journalists and reporters also travelling from one studio to another. It was mayhem for the security services. Luckily, at most entrances and checkpoints the security personnel knew me, thus enabling me to transport my passengers/guests through almost unhindered.

I was just about to call my controller to tell him that I wouldn't be able to complete the subsequent job due to the late appearance of my passenger. I had barely begun to dial when a woman burst into the back of my car, threw her handbag on the rear seat and sat herself down, slamming the door really hard. Because on many occasions, passengers who knew my car would simply jump in sometimes, I had to tell them that they were in the wrong car and as a precaution, I asked the lady if her name was Barbara and if her destination was St Albans. "Yes, and you are late," was all she said. I was taken aback by her abrasiveness and became cautious so as not to get into an argument.

Being a self-employed sub-contractor, I sometimes had to swallow some unpleasant and harsh words. I didn't have to, but the business I was in was very well paid and I almost always managed to avoid any confrontation well before it could even develop. One of the tricks I had learned was to install an engine cut off switch so that the car 'wouldn't start'. I used this technique only twice and did it regretfully but it was only to protect myself from any disputes going any further. My biggest problem was being late, but that wasn't down to me, it was mainly down to the controllers who gave me the wrong pick up times. I also had to learn how to turn down some of the jobs, because there was no time to reach the passenger on time and I just didn't want to take all the flak on too many occasions.

There is a difference between minicab driving and limousine chauffeur driving. My job was to drive a lot of 'high powered' people and foreign diplomats and escort them to different venues. There were times when I had to use my public relation skills to complete the job for which I was handsomely remunerated. When there was a V.I.P job, I allowed myself at least 15-20 minutes extra time, just to be punctual. My explanation about that switch may sound harsh but sometimes I had to be prepared to use this technique in order to protect my dignity. I certainly never had to think about using that switch whilst driving any of the V.I.P's. Those V.I.P passengers had common sense and believed the reason why I was running 2-5 minutes late, which was also often down to heavy traffic.

I didn't consider Barbara as a V.I.P and after I pressed that switch, the engine was still running! I realised that I would have to drive her after all! As an ex tour guide my diplomacy and tact cut in again. I tried to diffuse the situation about my passenger's rudeness straight away. The quick introduction of myself worked. I knew that she was quite an important employee because the car was taking her to and from her home on a regular basis at BBC expense, but waiting time had to be paid for by her. There were ways to persuade most of the passengers who were late, that my business consisted of three things: Driving, taking some of my passengers on foot to some places and waiting. The office warned me about this lady passenger and to not take her comments seriously and that she liked to play 'psychological games' with every driver. I wasn't ready for any of her games.

My car doors were very sophisticated and any excessive force on the door handles or slamming them could cause malfunction and the repairs were very costly. My knowledge of London roads and places was comprehensive and in no time, we reached the M1 motorway quickly via the back streets of North London. By now the rain was really pelting down.

The lady asked me if I was Irish (the polite way of asking where my accent was from). Unfortunately, she couldn't figure out where Slovenia was. By mentioning the former Yugoslavia she began to talk about how she travelled through part of Montenegro many years ago. I could see that she relaxed a bit and asked if I knew where she lived in St Albans. Of course I knew, because her address was logged on my GPS beforehand. It didn't bother me on that occasion that she was only 10 minutes late because we progressed well and there would be enough time left for me to go to the next pickup point afterwards without any delay. The rain appeared to be even more intense. We exchanged a few more words and my concentration was on the traffic ahead.

As we passed the sign for Scratch Wood Service Station, I noticed a rumbling noise coming from the back of the car. I knew it was a puncture and came to a halt just at the exit to the service station. Barbara asked anxiously why we had stopped. Her question told me that she obviously didn't drive. My reply was: "We have a puncture." I could see that she had become very nervous and she asked me to continue driving towards the service area. I just kept quiet and switched on the hazard lights and walked some 50 yards and placed the warning triangle in place. I could feel the driving rain seeping down my neck. "Zinco, can you please drive further down the slip road." I decided not to go into any technical details about the possible damage my alloy wheel would receive if I did drive further. The explanation that we were no longer on the motorway, but on a slip road leading to the service station was in vain. I also pointed out that the car was hard to manoeuvre with a flat tyre, hence we could end up in the ditch. Barbara demanded that she talk to the booking office. My phone was handed to her and she finally got through to the dispatcher and began shouting down the line about how inconsiderate I was and many other silly little lies about my conduct in the situation we found ourselves in. The controller asked her to hand my phone back to me and he asked that I do my best to get her home as soon as possible. It would take a RAC roadside assistance mechanic more than two hours to get to me. The controller estimated it would take over an hour for another car and driver to reach the point where I was stuck. I made a silly mistake anyway by moving the car slightly forward and both near side front and rear wheels were now on the grass verge only because I tried to placate Barbara. Finally, Dave, the controller said that Barbara had complained about every driver to date and any complaints about me were the least of my worries and I should have just let him know when I would be on the road again.

It took me some twenty minutes to replace the wheel in total darkness but through all the years of driving around the UK and beyond and having many punctures in the process, I was quite pleased with myself and we were soon on our way towards Barbara's home. She wouldn't say a word for a good while. She couldn't care less that I was cold and wet. Even when I tried to put the heater on she told me not to as she felt hot. Deep inside I just wondered what kind of a woman she was.

As we stopped at her house Barbara still insisted that I had put her in a dangerous and precarious situation back at the spot where we stopped and that she would make a formal complaint about me. I felt that enough was enough and told her calmly that it would be me who would complain about her since our conversation and her shouting was recorded! Which of course it wasn't. Without any further ado she got out of my car and slammed the door again.

As I headed back towards London my phone rang and the dispatcher said that Barbara rang him and wanted to apologise about her behaviour, obviously worried about my complaints about her to her superiors. All I said was that the office should not book me to drive Barbara ever again. Back at home my little dog, a Yorkie called Duke, was obviously waiting for me to arrive home. One of my neighbours would normally take him out about three hours before my return which was usually around 11-11.30pm.

Once indoors I was shivering but Duke had to be fed and taken out for a few minutes and then off to bed but I ended up with pneumonia and I didn't work for the next few days. The experience with Barbara really affected me and I decided to stay in my junk shop in Brick Lane for a few days. Brick Lane turned into one of London's biggest street markets every Sunday and the takings were enough to keep me going without doing any driving for the next ten days. Every week I would go around the auction houses and buy new stock. It wasn't all junk. Some Victoriana, Art Deco, Georgian and continental objects of art.

Soon the office rang me and asked if I was prepared to take on some work. "Of course," I replied. They booked me the journey with the parliamentarian and politician Tony Benn to Manchester and back to London. Mr Benn was expected to make a speech at BBC Conference Centre, and I had enough spare time to spend in Manchester. I had just bought myself a fish and chips lunch, sat down in the park, when my phone began to ring. It was the office and my phone fell to the ground because of my greasy fingers. They rang again and asked if I could talk. "I am all ears" was my reply. It was the same controller-dispatcher whom I spoke with on the night I had my puncture and about Barbara's complaints. He sounded very cheerful and queried if I wanted to earn some extra money for the next four nights in a row. The passenger will be driven on each night at 9pm from TV studios in Wood Lane to St Albans. "If it is Barbara Dave, just forget it!" He realised that I was serious about not driving Barbara again, and added that the office thought highly of me. "Zinco, (it was my nickname, namely short for Zdenko) Barbara could bring a lot of her colleagues from her department to book all their travelling with our office and by the way, it would be good if they could see me the next day at the office" and rang off.

They hadn't seen me for a good while, since all the bookings, the hours and daily sheets were completed by phone or fax. The manager came straight to the point and congratulated me on the way I handled Barbara. Apparently, she had never asked for a driver with whom she had had a spat, to drive her again. They made me look important since there was a chance of Barbara bringing us more work. Although the booking office was owned by the BBC, the employees were able to use other cab companies as well. I agreed and wanted to see how it would all work out.

On the next evening at 9 o'clock I was outside the studios and waited. Barbara came out about fifteen minutes late. I thought 'here we go again,' her being late and reading me my rights once more. She apologised and surprisingly offered payment for the waiting time. I declined her offer politely and decided to give her an inside view of how my business and most cab firms operate. "Waiting time is not enough for me to sustain the business," I went on, "and there were approximately 5-6 journeys a day allocated to me. There is no time to do any more. When the customer is very late, I have to cancel my next appointment journey which could have been a well- paid long- distance job." She admitted that she never thought about that and added that she was always under the impression that we drivers just want to extract more money from the customers. Surprisingly she saw the point. Coincidentally we were approaching the same spot where we had to stop to change the rear wheel two weeks ago. Suddenly she asked me to turn into the service station as she had to visit the loo. It was my last job and I politely said: "Your wish is my command!"

After about fifteen minutes she came back with two cups of coffee. She looked happy and offered me one cup and sat herself in the front seat which I didn't mind. She then wanted me to move the car to a quiet spot where there were no bright lights. To my surprise, she then out of blue said that I was the only one who dared to challenge her on that night with the puncture. She kept asking me if I was married, have any children and if I had my own property. The questions seemed to me out of place since some two weeks ago she wanted to report me to her head office and now all this sudden niceness. Little bells were ringing in my head and telling me to place the cup in the car cup holder and to continue the journey.

I started the engine and was just about to move on and turn the front dim cabin light off, when Barbara suddenly asked to stop, which I did. As I turned my head towards her, she had pulled up her skirt, spread her legs wide open, with no underwear and asked with a soft voice "Do you want some?" I was totally unprepared for the situation and blurted out a few words which meant in all honesty nothing. In short, I got scared even thinking about touching her, especially after what had happened on the night when I first drove her and her threats. I fought off the thought of the temptation to engage in any sexual act with that woman, mainly because of fear of what she would do afterwards. At that time, I was in a brief relationship with Julia in Teddington and had been with her the week before. Being a typical Taurian man, we Taurians by tradition hardly ever two-time women.

Yes, Barbara was very attractive, but I just didn't trust her, fearing possible accusation of attempted or actual rape of a BBC employee. She noticed my hesitation and asked me if I was a gay. I said "No" and just wanted to get out of the situation as quickly as possible. I must say again, she was very attractive and most certainly, there were many men after her. We chatted throughout the rest of the journey as if nothing out of the ordinary had happened. An opportunity arose to tell her that my aunty in Slovenia was very ill and that she would have another driver until my return.

When we arrived outside her house Barbara asked me again if I wanted to come into her house and have a hot drink. I had to resist the temptation and kept thinking about her behaviour on the first night. There was also another reason, my little dog Duke, who had to be taken out and fed. We said good night and off I went.

The M1 was clear and very soon I was in West London and home. Duke was going frantic and nudged me to take him for a little walk. Upon our return my phone was ringing, and the caller's number showed up on the display. It was not a London number. It kept ringing till the auto- answering cut in. The message was from Barbara and it said that she would like to see me before my trip to Slovenia. Then my girlfriend Julia rang and asked me to come and see her the next day. Julia was a head teacher at one of the primary schools in Teddington, Surrey. She had two boys aged fifteen and seventeen. Her sons were very well behaved and liked my stories about my life as a BBC driver. They obviously wanted to know more about some TV celebrities and personalities, but for me that was off limits. No exceptions.

I was issued with a Public Carriage office certificate which meant that CRB (criminal record bureau office) had done all the enhanced checks on me, regarding any criminal records for the last thirty years and beyond. Of course, that was a prerequisite to be able to join the BBC Corporation as a subcontractor in the first place. My experience as an approved driving instructor some ten years prior was another reason that the BBC Corporation accepted me to join them. Julia wanted to take our relationship to the next level, but I loved my freedom, considering that I had two failed marriages and three engagements behind me, which all 'ended in tears' so to speak.

That phone call from Barbara bugged me for the rest of the evening. I decided not to contact her until my return from the forthcoming trip. Why was she phoning me? Why did she expose herself on that evening? What would happen if we ended up in bed and things didn't turn out the way I wanted? She could even ruin my reputation with some lies about me. I was a fifty two year old man, not looking my age, well presented, single and wearing expensive suits. I also had my own flat in West London's Bayswater and had a lease of a second- hand shop in East London, so why would a woman like Barbara want to see me, after her threats to report me. I must reiterate, she was in her early forties, very attractive, nearly a foot taller than me, had a son who was a University of Durham graduate and according to her, owned a terraced house in St Albans. The more I thought about it the more I wanted to forget about her and her advances. She was therefore, in my mind 'deleted' for ever.

Meeting The MP Tony Benn

What I loved most about the business I was in, was the freedom to choose the names of my passengers well in advance, and was glad, that I knew, that Mr Tony Benn would have to be driven back to London. It all went well without any motorway closures leading out of Manchester. He was really tired and slept for most of the time. Almost all of the controllers and dispatchers knew about my shop and knew that, unless there were jobs which would yield a good income, I would go elsewhere. On one occasion I did join a third company for a short while and drove customers coming mainly from the MOD (Ministry of Defence). The company was based in Docklands, and their jobs started at 3am and I would have to bring the same customer back at the end of the day. I would be paid by the minutes and hours spent on each job, rather than by the mileage, but the contract tied me down too much and I wasn't able to be in my shop Sundays. I hadn't aimed to become a '007 agent' although without a doubt, many of my passengers were MI5-MI6 personnel for that matter. I re-joined the BBC and renewed my contract again. From then on, the office manager understood that I had to earn decent money in order to maintain my expensive car, which was using a lot of petrol and pay for very costly insurance (Group 34 or higher).

At the very beginning I took a lot of advice from other drivers who had been doing the same job for years. I noticed that they would sometimes 'give it a miss' to certain destinations and certain passengers, although those jobs-journeys appeared to be well paid. Later on, I found out why and it transpired that they often had bad experiences with some of the lesser known celebrities, who would refuse to sign the waiting time. The waiting time was subsequently connected to the airport's extortionate costs of parking while waiting and that wouldn't be paid either and they would end up being underpaid.

There was one other lady passenger who I 'deleted from my books,' Y. A. Beige. I drove her on a few occasions and every time she wanted to unfold my daily sheet and have a 'perusal' of whom I drove on that day so that she could mention some of the names on the programs she took part in. On that evening I was determined to put a stop to it and this time, as she went for that daily sheet the moment she got into the car, I had a split second to snatch it from her hand. She became extremely unpleasant and no matter what I did to ease the situation, she continuously wanted to change the route and almost shouted: "Do you know London at all, you stupid foreigner!" At that remark, I had had enough of her verbal insults and replied that she was a foreigner herself, hiding behind her Anglo-Saxon surname of Beige! (her real name withheld) I was determined to teach her a lesson, regardless of the possible repercussions and about a quarter of a mile from the studios in Wood Lane, I stopped the car and pretended to start the engine a few more times. At the same time, I rang my controllers and left the phone off the hook for the controller to hear her abusive language. She went on ranting and rambling for some fifteen minutes, left the car and went to hail a black cab. Not a single cab stopped, and she finally had to walk the last two hundred and fifty yards towards the studios. I felt disappointed at losing a customer and the fare. She didn't mention anything about our spat to the programme producer. By the way, she is still famous to this day for her rudeness and I still switch the telly off whenever her face is shown. Never ever had anyone whilst working with BBC called me a stupid foreigner.

There were different circumstances, when someone would refer to me as a 'foreigner' but it was said in a joking way and totally harmless. Maybe, had my BBC contract been the main source of income, I would be forced to put up with that lady's verbal insults. There were times, when I drove some of the BBC employees to one of the three main London airports. The corporation rate was anywhere between £60 and £90. On one occasion I picked up a family, where the mother worked for the Corporation and I had driven her on one occasion. I knew that her children where going to travel with them, but what I didn't know was that their children would soon begin to play with various switches and sophisticated buttons on each of the doors, such as window control, rear heating or air conditioning, rear dimmed lights, on the refrigerated middle console and the rest. I waited for them to stop, but they didn't. Then, there was at the same time their mother also 'fiddling' with the car radio, which itself didn't bother me. I, in a calm voice, made their mother aware that there was a danger of a malfunction if the children continued to randomly wind the electric windows up and down. The mother's answer was: "Up to now, my children always used to touch those buttons, and what's the fuss?" I had to pause and think what to reply and said in a few words how expensive repairs were and that the car is still on HP (loan) and how I understood that children do get bored. "I thought the car belonged to the BBC and that you are just a driver." There was no need for me to say another word and she made her kids stop pressing those buttons, but I also knew that she wouldn't drive with me again and she didn't. I had no choice but to be firm, because no garage would replace any of those switches or electrical motors for less than £200 and I had sadly lost her as a customer.

The next day I had to prepare my car for the arduous 1200 miles trip to Slovenia. The car was a top of the range Mercedes 320 S class. There was still a small outstanding balance of payments left. According to my accountant it was supposed to be wise to owe some money to the bank because it is then offset in my tax returns. My little Duke was taken to my neighbours and I was on my way. The next stop was my shop to collect some items for some of my relatives. The Dover docks formalities were straight forward and the boarding began straight away.

Once I was parked on the ferry I went to the restaurant. I was looking forward to having my favourite meal: Fish and chips with mushy peas, pickled gherkin and some ketchup topped with tartare sauce - yummy. Disembarking went even faster and the route out of Calais was well known to me. France had some months before, introduced stiffer penalties for any serious speeding, therefore I set the speed limiter to 70mph and the time and miles just flew by. After leaving the Brussels orbital motorway, which is similar to our M25, the petrol guzzling car needed a refill. There were a lot of hitch hikers asking me for a 'lift' but, I had to say no to all of them because my insurance policy wouldn't cover me in the event of an accident or theft through having a hitch hiker on board.

There were some really nice places to be found along the way only two to three miles from the motorway. I just wanted to have a nice room at any of the small guest houses with a homemade meal and some local wine. It would save time not to drive through the towns and end up in some Novotel or other of the impersonal hotels. It took me five minutes to find a small guest house with adjoining restaurant and a neon lit sign: Rooms - vacancy. The price was 30 Euros for a single room.

I took the room straight away and soon found myself in the restaurant ordering local fare. Having no moral obligation to Julia back in UK, I eyed a nice lady serving me. During my meal I kept looking at her and she every so often looked in my direction.

After I ordered some wine she came to my table and introduced herself and asked me whether the meal was satisfactory for me. It is common on the continent that managers or proprietors would come and sit with a customer and chat with them. My intention was to come back and chat her up. A man appeared soon afterwards and spoke to her in German, which I speak fluently, as to how she should look after other customers as well. She stood up and gave me a forlorn look and left my table.

The phone rang and it was Barbara, and I wondered how she got my second number. She asked in a chirpy voice how the traffic was in Germany. She added that my booking office gave her my second number and was told that I was one of their best drivers with many prominent customers on my books, including Jeremy Paxman, Clive James and so on. She revealed that she knew a lot of phones' ringtones due to her line of work. She finished the conversation with how she already missed me.

My poor aunty was suffering really badly and after I visited my extensive family, (eight aunties and their families) and gave their grandchildren some little presents, I went back to the hospital to see her again. Deep inside I had a feeling that she wasn't going to make it. It was a short trip and I was soon UK bound on Austrian and German motorways.

After another day of driving I arrived back in Dover and late at night collected Duke from my neighbour. I took him for a long walk and on return my phone was ringing. It was Julia who wanted to know why I hadn't rung her all this time. She wanted to know if there was something that she should know about our relationship. I said politely that we had no relationship. We saw each other once a month and it should stay like that. She put the phone down. I wasn't proud of what was said but I was as honest as I could be. The phone rang again and as I thought that it was Julia, it went unanswered.

Just before being ready to go to bed I had an urge to play my piano. It was an upright piano with real ivory covered keys. It was bought at auction two years before and it sounded not much different from a Grand piano. To my horror I noticed that my playing was getting very rusty. Instruments like this must be played, if possible, daily. The next morning my phone woke me up and it was Barbara. It went through my mind not to answer it but after two more rings I, in a nice way, reminded her that she should wait until I rang her and ended the call. I hoped that she would get the message and went back to sleep. A whole pile of letters had to be read and dealt with. Some of them were final notices for payments despite having a direct debit set up with my bank and sufficient money deposited. Upon contacting my bank, I learned that there was an error caused by me. Inadvertently I set up direct debits on my sole trader account instead of on a personal account. In the end, it was all sorted and I could concentrate on my work. The next job was to take Hugh Edwards, the newscaster, to the studios. It was always a pleasure to drive him around London and I did this on many occasions. We often discussed a bit about our private lives, not any intimate discussions, but about energy bills, the 'rip off' garages, internet hacking and so on.

2

Meeting Prince Andrew & Many More

Interesting People

The next job flagged up on the mobile was to take Frank Gardner, a war correspondent, to the Duke of York, Prince Andrew's residence near Windsor. It was called a wait and return trip, which could last anything between three hours and a whole day. I found that nobody at the gates, from the security, body- searched me or my car and I was thrilled that BBC put so much trust in me! The whole place looked like a scene from a fairy tale.

Mr Gardner indicated that should I decide to stay and wait, the servants would look after me regarding my lunch, or alternatively, I could go somewhere else for a few hours. I decided to stay and enjoy the Duke's hospitality.

The whole experience was unforgettable. There was an array of trays with all sorts of sandwiches, coffee, tea, hot chocolate, seemingly for some dignitaries and I really felt like a VIP! I asked one of the staff, who looked like a CID man in plain clothes, if there was a chance for me to sit on one of the benches not far from the residence's entrance and have my lunch there. He just smiled and politely told me that I could. Later on, I discovered that most probably HM The Queen sat there in her childhood. The bench looked to me old enough then. It took Mr Gardner nearly 3 hours to finish his interview and he himself possibly had a quick lunch with the Duke. Mr Gardner lost his ability to walk in the Middle East as a war correspondent where he was badly injured in both his legs and was wheelchair bound but had never allowed himself to be wheeled around. After a good while, they both finally appeared and made their way towards my car. I will never forget the moment when Prince Andrew came closer to me and greeted me and shook my hand. He asked me where I was from and how did I like the UK. After we exchanged a few more words, Mr Gardner quickly said that I was writing a book and I then added that he, The Prince, would also be mentioned. The Prince smiled and added that he would be interested to read the book. Such a shame I didn't just ask him where to send my upcoming book to. Mr Gardner was my very special client and especially for what he had been through. A true hero! Meanwhile my phone went unanswered a few times knowing it came from Barbara.

My next booking was to take Ms Ruby Wax to the West End to do some shopping. It took us a few hours and Ms Wax was very polite and courteous towards me. She commented that she liked my bow tie. I always wore a bow tie just to show that my job took priority. Occasionally there were other passengers asking me why I wore a bow tie and my answer was always the same: it was 'for them to feel important.' In general, they just laughed at my comments. I acquired a new Nokia mobile which also had a facsimile facility therefore there was no need to go back to the office to collect the dockets for the next day and it saved me a lot of time.

The next job to appear on my new mobile fax machine was Barbara's, to take her home the next evening. It went through my head how to avoid at all costs to have to drive her again. Even my call to the office didn't help. Derek, one of the dispatchers, joked that he would take her had he been allowed. "You are welcome to her" was my reply. Although I had a contract with two other companies, my allegiance was with the BBC which gave me most of the work. Niven, a well- known PCO certified company, had its main contract with BBC transport and was my second favourite firm to work with. I was classed as their 'A1' driver. After a few minutes of consideration, I decided to show some loyalty to my office and accepted to take Barbara home to St Albans the next evening.

The following day passed relatively easy. Mr Ken Livingstone had a long meeting at the Houses of Parliament and the waiting time amounted to some 3 hours. After taking him back to TV studios in Wood Lane I was calculating that my earnings were quite good. Incidentally after a month or so, I had just dropped off Mr Benn at the Houses of Parliament when I spotted Mr Livingstone, hopping with his left leg in plaster, across the road. I stopped just before the pedestrian crossing and stepped out of the car and said: "Hello Mr Livingstone, I'll take you back to your office, without charge."

He looked at me for a second and replied: "Aah, it's you, the Slovene from the BBC, let's clear the road," and with that he sat himself on the back seat. It was only a half a mile trip and he wanted to pay but I refused and wished him a nice day and drove off.

I had enough time to have a light supper at the TV studios restaurant. The cost of meals was very low in comparison to local restaurants, because it was subsidised by the Corporation. The clock was ticking away, and I made my way to the front of studios' main entrance to be on time for Barbara's arrival. She came on time. She thanked me for taking her home, pointing out that she sensed that I was trying to avoid her. We drove off taking the same route as before.

She then asked how my aunty was and if the journey was tiresome. She was talking non- stop about her son and her father who was in a care home not far from where she lived. I was just listening and tried to build some kind of a picture of her. The more she was telling me the more I struggled to come to a conclusion about what kind of a person she was. To be honest I couldn't make head or tail of anything she talked about. We approached her address and I was caught by surprise as she asked me to come in for a coffee or tea. I followed her into her house to have a hot cuppa and thought, why not? The house was in need of fresh décor, but it looked clean. I had to take into consideration that she was a single mother and as far as I could see she was a hard worker. She paid for her son's university fees and boarding. We sat on the sofa and chatted for a while.

She behaved completely opposite to the way she had on our previous journey. Barbara didn't spread her legs, didn't take off her panties and in short, she acted just like any woman I had a coffee with in their homes. Instead she wanted to know more about me and my life. I wasn't going to be read like an open book. On my mind was still the night when we had a puncture and her threat with the forthcoming complaint to her superiors and also her promiscuous proposition a short while after that. I asked myself, how many other drivers were also lucky to have her attention? Time passed ever so quickly and it was time for me to go and I said that it was nice of her to offer me a coffee and with that went through the door, started my car and drove off. It wasn't the thought of how many men she probably seduced in their cars that put me off. It was the malicious threat that she made on that first journey. It didn't take long to get home where Duke was waiting for me patiently.

He had been on his own for about three hours. There was enough time to take him to Hyde Park for a long walk. It also gave me time to think about Barbara. Why did she invite me to her house? Why all this attention? What was she expecting from me? There was a little detail that I remembered whilst drinking coffee back at her house. She nearly tripped over an electric cable. Somehow, she just didn't lift her leg despite looking at it. My immediate thought was that she was on drugs of some sort, but her speech wasn't slurred to indicate that she was under influence of any. Duke wanted to go home and after I parked my car in the garage below and opened the front door the phone rang and it was Julia asking me to come to Teddington to collect the few items I had left in her house. It gave me an indication that she realised our brief relationship was over. I was glad since she didn't like my adorable pet in her house anyway. Duke was my pet and a friend and what was the point for me to leave Duke in London instead of him being with me. Besides that, I often felt guilty to leave him with my neighbours for hours on end. I thought that at that moment it was the right time to tell her what I thought.

She just asked me if my dog Duke meant more to me than her and I said "Yes," adding that in the event we would go any further she would demand that I give Duke away. "Duke is my friend and he will stay with me for as long as he lives" were my last words. Duke was an exceptionally cute little dog. During my Sunday trading in Brick Lane I had people coming to my shop to stroke him and give him some of his favourite treats.

Sometimes I wanted to clear some of my stock and so secured a pitch at Portobello market near Notting Hill Gate W11 where many people would take a photo of my Duke sitting in the shopping basket fixed on the bike's handlebar.

I felt sorry that things didn't work out as Julia expected, and on a few occasions, she mentioned that I was sometimes a bit 'stuck up.' Her reasons for saying that, was my request to see the kitchen of a very expensive restaurant before ordering a meal. But what she forgot, although I had told her about my catering experience in Switzerland, was this fact: "If the chef's clothes and shoes are filthy, the food won't be much different."

On many occasions, during my entire life, I was wrongly perceived as being too choosy, acting 'posh', a bit arrogant and oversensitive. None of the above is true. I just wanted to achieve more in my life, never to return to the way of life in my teens when I had to run away from home due to my father's cruelty towards me. During those turbulent times, whilst looking for somewhere to sleep, I also had to leave in the middle of the night and my so called 'peers', on whose sofa or bed I slept, because they were involved in burglaries and other crimes. I just didn't want to take part in their activities. Period.

The Labour party had a conference in Blackpool and the fax sent to me early in the morning had outlined my itinerary in detail and again, my passenger was Mr Tony Benn. He lived in a leafy Holland Park Avenue West London and he was always courteous towards me. He showed me the Houses of Parliament and once even took me to one of the bars, of course not to drink with him but just to show me where he had an occasional pint. On that morning and on our way towards Blackpool I popped a question, why had he chosen me to be his chauffeur for two days? He paused a little and said that he would like to know more about my life in the then Yugoslavia and my botched attempt to illegally cross the border to Austria. He paused again and mentioned the incident when after a previous journey he left behind his wallet, with all of his credit cards, some cash and various security entry badges. "You," he went on, "Zdenko, you delivered that wallet to my home 'in a flash' and I didn't even have time to give you a tip since you left in such a hurry. Don't leave in a hurry tomorrow and besides you are driving like the wind, so effortlessly without a sign of any nervousness and knowing that you were a driving instructor I feel safe." Well, I felt honoured, but still had to keep the distance as not to go over the threshold between me as his driver and him as a distinguished politician. Many of our drivers didn't or couldn't understand why many customers asked for me. I presume, it was just because my approach towards them was always diplomatic and courteous, non-inquisitive, and above all, without any 'stage fright', regardless whether they be movie stars, diplomats, corporate chairmen or politicians.

Some of my clients would talk to me and some wouldn't say much. Most of them liked my common sense approach, non-inquisitive nature and the fact I didn't ever comment about other passengers. My daily sheet was designed to have space for the signature confirming any waiting times or de-routings. It inadvertently showed to every passenger whom I had driven on that day and I had to be prepared for any possible questions. The hardest bit was to fend off some of the media executives, who were persistently wanting to know who my other customers were. With some of them being journalists, they of course saw an opportunity to hear some of my stories and especially wanted to hear some bad stories. Mr Crawford (the real name omitted) was a perfect example and an epitome of a typical inquisitive journalist-publicist. In no way, am I implying any improprieties, and am merely citing the questions he came up with: "Where did Mr, Ms, Mrs, go? What were they saying?" These were the most common questions, but I had to use all my PR skills to avoid going into any details and at the same time keep him happy. There is nothing more to say about Mr Crawford other than his 'clever try' to gain some information connected to my passengers failed. He had subsequently served a prison sentence for 'interfering with the evidence.' On two occasions I was offered sums of money by some other executives of well-known media companies, to gather some information on some of the VIP's and that didn't work with me either. It was simply an offer to spy on my passengers.

Because of the above mentioned daily sheet's design, I racked my brain how to develop a way to avoid those passenger names being visible, while signing my daily sheet, so they wouldn't be able to see whom I drove on that day. I ended up with folding the daily sheet into three parts so that there were only 2-3 passenger's names visible. Any other VIP names would then be hidden within the folded daily sheet, but later on I refined it even further.

If any of the passengers decided to pursue such a question like: 'What restaurant did he or she go to?' I would politely say that they wouldn't be happy if they ever heard my comments about themselves. It usually worked!

I could at this stage write about something which DIDN'T happen, for example, how Mr Benn divulged information about his work as a politician and his private life. To write about that, would be wrong.

After we arrived at the destination and all the waiting time and miles were signed, Mr Benn then thrust a £50 note into my hand and said: "Well done Zdenko. I'll see you in a while." He did and after two days I had to go back to Blackpool and bring him back home to London. He was tired and mostly slept during the journey, a sure sign that he felt safe.

Another two months passed and the stock in my shop was getting low and I had to cancel all the journeys for the following day. Luckily there were only two local journeys booked and I forgot to tell my booking office to cancel them both. It caused a small problem for my controllers, nevertheless. It was an auction day at the West London Philips auction house and the auction room was heaving with buyers. The chance to buy something for the price that would yield a profit after all the expenses, looked slim. My limit to bid for something worthwhile was somewhere between £2000 -£3000. Slowly lots were selling one by one for the price much higher than estimated. There were other lots sold which were too pricey for my clientele in Brick Lane. I decided to bid for three boxes 3ft by 4ft full of lead crystal cut chandelier pieces. They looked quite old and the wrapping told me that they probably came from a closed down factory.

After a few hours of frantic bidding for other lots there were only three lots left and only a small group of people were left. I thought surely there will be something to bid for with my budget.

The lot with those three huge boxes was eventually called out. The bidding price was £500. I looked around and recognised that there were two bidders bidding for the same lot as myself. I recognised them as being two antique shop owners in Kensington Church Street West London. The three of us began bidding. £550, £600, £650, £720, £790, £840, and I ended up with a risk of making a loss and made a final bid of £3650! The two shop owners came to me and asked if I knew what I was bidding for. I put on my brave face and said "Yes," knowing that it was my 'bluff.' They offered me £130 for a few items which they were after. I told them that it was too soon since my head was spinning a bit but gave them my phone number and told them to ring me in a couple of days. They left a bit disappointed. By then there was only me at the cashier's window and I paid in full and in cash. There were 3 porters already waiting to help me with those 'supposed three boxes. They asked me to follow them to their huge storage hall at the back and asked me what kind of car I was driving and pointed at my second car, a German version of Range Rover. They led me to some 15 boxes of the same size that were in the sale room and full to the brim with the same chandelier pieces! I went quiet and blurted out that I would like to go and see those three boxes still in the sale room to check. I followed them to those boxes and began to read again the notes stuck on the top of the boxes saying in the small print: Part lot of number........

Bingo! I just realised that those two shopkeepers like me had overlooked the small print below the bidding number. I was over the moon. The Auction House was only some two miles away from my place and the garage. My calculation was that there would be three journeys needed. I offered one of the porters £30 pounds for each journey to help me unload all those boxes into my garage. I knew that I was onto a winner in a big way. I wondered what those two dealers' reactions would be had they seen the rest of that lot. Lastly, I wasn't envious that they had expensive articles in their shops in the least, but I wanted to earn some money as well. I spent the next few days shifting 8 of those boxes to my shop in Brick Lane. The phone was ringing non-stop. Barbara wanted to be driven home by me, the two antique dealers wanted to buy all the stock and the booking office wondered when I would be available again since they were extremely busy.

I needed to find out what the value was of the crystal cut chandelier pieces and decided to reserve a pitch in Portobello market for the following Saturday. The weather was perfect on that day and it took me some time to load my big G wagon and in the company of Duke I arrived early to secure a parking space for the day. I nearly broke my back trying to carry 4 huge boxes to my pitch. In the end I had to ask two passers-by to give me a hand. I gave them £15 each for their help.

By 6am the stall was set up with only those crystals and it looked like something out of an Aladdin's cave. The sun's rays caused the glass pieces to glitter in all the rainbow colours. All that was needed was customers. Within half an hour there was a huge crowd around my stall. There were German, Italian, French antique dealers and of course the majority were British. I didn't know what to charge for each piece. Some were 4" some were 10" long. Some were round, some were of triangular shape, some were spherical, some square and others short. I started with a price of

£4 for a small piece and £10 for larger pieces. In no time I had some £500 pounds in my pocket. Next to my stall was a lady selling some second-hand clothes. I offered her £40 to help me wrap up each item sold when she wasn't busy with her customers. I had met her before and she was very helpful indeed. She even pointed out that some of the customers were trying to steal some of the items.

I told her of my awareness of some of the things 'missing' and took it as collateral damage, being a street trader. Money was rolling in and within three hours I reckoned I already had my money back and felt elated! Obviously, I wasn't stupid enough to take any money out of my bulging pockets which were filled with notes. Suddenly there was somebody tapping me on my shoulder and there were those two dealers who approached me at the Auction house. They looked very disappointed that I didn't call them. I just said that I had to find out what those crystals were worth and selling them to the open public was the best way. They went around my stall and began to pick up different pieces like the rest of the other customers. When they heard what I charged the next customer for each piece and how fast the things were selling, they realised that it was silly of them to think that I was some small-time market trader and that they would have to come out with a more realistic proposal than the proposition they made back at the Auction house. One of the female customers came closer to me and bluntly interrupted those two dealers and asked me how much I would charge for some 150 pieces of different shapes and sizes. I jokingly said that she must be involved with a holistic occult in some way. She nodded and asked how I knew. "It was only a guess" was my reply. I gave her an empty banana box and told her to go ahead and choose what she wanted. The two dealers were getting very nervous because they saw how well the sale was going. There were some Italian dealers and they wanted to buy some 80 pieces as well. "Holy cow"! I just couldn't believe my luck. I charged her £700 which was below the 'normal price'? (cheeky me!) and she paid without any hesitation.

I charged the Italians £400 and they paid without any haggling. I realised that maybe I had priced it too low but didn't want to change the prices until the next trading day. I know now that I was never greedy and people around me also knew it and sometimes took me for a ride. The phone rang many times but I was too busy and switched it off. The two dealers were still standing next to me and saw how fast the stock was disappearing and wanted to talk, but I had to serve my customers and told them to wait till the end since there were still 3 nearly full boxes under my stall. I noticed that they were getting a bit agitated because I showed them that there was no hurry for me to sell them the remaining 3 boxes straight away. I began to somehow have doubts about their intentions. They mentioned something about paying by cheque. Now I had to change the tone and so I told them that their comment about paying with a cheque sounds silly and they should know that street market trading is in cash, hoping that they would leave me alone. With that said I decided to pack up and go home. Duke was getting restless and hungry. I switched my phone back on again and the messages box was full, but nothing urgent.

I gave Lorna £40 and asked her to keep an eye on Duke and my wrapped boxes whilst I fetched my car. I covered them with a cloth. It took me 10 minutes to get back and position my car close to my stall. As I walked back towards my stall the two dealers were taking the bits out of the remaining boxes and examining them, which I didn't like because there were people beginning to do the same. I politely asked them not to interfere with my business and to stop taking my stock out of the already packed boxes. After their apology we agreed that they would come to my junk shop in Brick Lane on the following day, which was Sunday, with a reasonable proposition. I just didn't trust them to take them back to my place. I also wanted someone like my burly friend Arnold with me if a deal was going to be done. I also gave them my word that I would not have any of the crystals on the stall outside my shop before 10am. Surprisingly they knew where my shop was.

On the way back home, I stopped at an M&S shop and bought two huge ribeye steaks and a bottle of expensive red wine to celebrate the windfall of money earned on that day. Of course, one steak was for Duke. The next stop was Hyde Park to give Duke a good run. The dinner was quickly prepared and Duke just couldn't finish his in one go. Mine was scoffed in no time. The wine made me quite tipsy and I had to lie down. The phone rang and it was Barbara. She wanted to know when I would decide to drive her home again. I remember saying "hopefully never again." It was rude of me saying that but it was how I felt at that moment. She paused and then asked me if everything was all right with me. "I'll ring you tomorrow because you sound a bit tipsy" were her words and she rang off. The next call came from my office and Diane, the dispatcher, wanted to know for sure when I would be available again to do some work. She had a nice and a well-paid job lined up for me for the following Tuesday to go to France for two days with two reporters and a cameraman. It was about filming the refugee camp in Sangatte near Calais. I jumped at the offer and promised to pick up all the paperwork first thing on Monday. My reasonably good knowledge of French of which my office knew, helped to secure that well paid trip. Only then was I ready to empty all my pockets and began counting the cash. It took me some fifteen minutes. In total it was £3720! I was thrilled. Duke just looked at me when I began to sing. It sounded more like a croaking than singing. After setting the alarm clock for the early morning I finished the remaining wine and fell asleep.

Duke woke me up well before the alarm clock went off and we were on our way to London's East End. Arnold, my neighbour in Brick Lane, was already at work. I went to a bagel shop and bought 4 bagels filled with smoked salmon and soft cheese. An extra portion of just salmon was for Duke. I told Arnold about my two visitors who were coming to buy some crystal bits and would he mind being with me, while the money was changing hands so to speak. He just nodded and said: "any time for you and by the way, I like the way you treat your Duke." I just laughed and uttered words like: "Duke is my friend and gets and eats his food before me."

At around 10am the two dealers showed up in my shop and we started talking. It was my suggestion that we should at least know each others' names. The loudest one was Gary, whereas Joe was mainly listening and helped to take those three boxes outside the shop and began sorting those bits on the two stalls outside the shop. Only then I realised that they didn't properly check any of the three boxes before bidding for them in the auction room.

Before long there were people wanting to buy some of the

crystals, but I had to stick to my promise not to sell any before the offer was made by Gary and Joe for the job-lot. We covered the contents of the first box and continued with the second box. I worked out that there was a pattern, as each batch of different shaped pieces was wrapped in a different coloured paper. It looked as if there were 80 batches with 10 pieces each. I estimated that each of three boxes contained some 800 pieces. I made a quick calculation and wanted £8 a piece, being the middle price. Joe who spoke very little up till then offered me £12000 for the lot. I wanted £13000 but was willing to settle for £12500. Gary wanted to give me a cheque, but I told him again that it was out of the question. "Gary look, you know that I had to pay for this lot in cash, and will not accept any cheque, end of story" and went to continue to add more stuff on the stall. I just wouldn't budge and Arnold presumed that I had a problem and came over. He asked if I was all right. He knew them both as his occasional customers and told them that I was very reasonable with my request to be paid in cash. Joe had an idea and suggested that he would pay £500 as a deposit and they'd pay me the rest upon my delivery to their shop in Kensington Church Street West London. I didn't like the idea of going to deliver those three boxes on my own. I asked Arnold to come inside my shop to ask him something in private. I wanted to know how much he would charge to come with me to Kensington at the end of the day to do the delivery. He wanted nothing but I insisted that he should be paid £80 for his help and Joe would have to pay an extra £80. Joe and Gary agreed and gave me a deposit of £500 in cash. I gave them a receipt and told them that Arnold and I would be at their shop at around 4pm.

At the appointment time I rang the bell and Gary invited us into their shop. Arnold was a strong man but didn't like the idea of walking into their shop. I could see that somehow he didn't trust them. I too declined their invitation and wanted to finish the deal outside their shop. I wasn't worried if somebody saw me counting the money on the pavement. All my goods were legitimate and I wanted to do it my way. Arnold was surprised at my self-confidence. Arnold was as strong as an ox and lifted those three boxes out of the back of my G-waggon with ease. Joe briefly looked at them and went to their shop and came out with the £12000 in cash. Firstly, I wanted to see the money. I asked Joe to take one of the £50 notes out of the bank sealed wrapper. I had a pen which would only show if the bank note was a bad forgery. It wasn't a perfect way of testing but there was no other way to test it on Sunday. The banknotes looked used and Arnold indicated that they looked real to him. Gary gave me the rest of the envelopes each containing £1000 pounds. I prepared a receipt and went on counting the rest of the money. The sum was correct and Arnold took the boxes to the entrance of the shop. I asked them for an extra £80 for Arnold. Joe made a remark and said that I was a 'tough cookie.' I smiled and took the extra £80 and handed it to Arnold. Then I pointed out the price tag on one of their shop's displayed chandeliers. The price was £25000! Arnold burst out laughing and picked up Duke and sat himself in the car. I started the car and we left. Whilst driving Arnold back to Brick Lane my phone rang and it was Barbara. I couldn't talk and asked her to phone back in an hour.

As Arnold was stepping out of the car, he had the money that I had given him in his hand and put it onto my lap and just said that I

should buy Duke some more salmon! He just didn't want to accept my £80! "I owe you a favour" were my words and I drove off again.

Barbara rang me back again and although it wasn't an offence back then to talk on the phone whilst driving, I briefly stopped and answered it. She sounded distressed and I asked if she was OK. She just couldn't get up and was waiting for an ambulance to take her to the nearest hospital. I asked again what was wrong with her. She just said that she was sorry that she was so rude on our first journey and hung up. I was too tired to venture all the way up to St Albans and didn't even know which hospital she would be admitted to. As usual Duke had to be taken for a walk to any park along the route. I parked my car in the garage and checked the second garage in case someone had broken into it. Although nobody ever tampered with any of my garage doors, nevertheless there was always a chance of it happening since I was often away during the day. My neighbours had a key to my maisonette and Duke was taken out regularly during my absence and I made sure that they were paid for that. The shop takings for that day were very good and Duke had the second half of the steak from the night before. I was satisfied with all the money and was suddenly toying with the idea to replacing my existing S Class Mercedes limo for the latest version.

I remembered my accountant's advice not to pay for a new car outright, but take out a loan, which is then offset with my yearly tax returns. I didn't like to have large sums of money lying around my place. My decision was to wait till the next day which was Monday and the cash was to be deposited at my bank and with that I fell asleep.

My phone woke me up and looking at the grandfather's clock

it was 4am. Who could be ringing me at this time of the night? It was Barbara ringing me from Watford General Hospital. I could tell that her voice was expressing anxiety and she sounded worried and frightened at the same time. She asked me if I could do her a favour and I said that it would depend on what kind of favour would that be, obviously not wanting to commit myself to something that I couldn't or wouldn't do. She needed some of her personal items from her house to be brought to her. I told her that I had a few driving jobs to do and that she should try to contact her brother who lived only a few miles away, but she explained briefly that her brother was in some kind of a home for people who could not cope with life on their own. It told me everything that she had nobody to give her any assistance at that point in time. I was in a terrible dilemma. I was asked by a woman who was going to report me for an alleged rudeness a while ago, to suddenly drop everything that I was doing and drive to Watford General Hospital. From there on to St Albans, pick up the items Barbara needed and drive back again to the hospital. After that I would have to drive myself back home to West London. I just didn't know what to do. I told Barbara that I would ring her back in a short while. I calculated that it would take me some 4-5 hours of driving and who knows, possibly be accused of stealing something from her house. I rang my office manager for his opinion and advice. He suggested that Barbara signs a waiver of some sort so that at least there would be something in writing. He asked me if I wanted to cancel the jobs booked for the day. I agreed and rang Barbara and gave her an approximate time of arrival and how she should in the meanwhile write on a piece of paper, an authorisation for me to go into her house. She couldn't

40

thank me enough and said that she would reimburse me for my loss of earnings for that day or at least for the hours I would spend on the road. I got dressed and left Duke with my neighbours, went to the bank and deposited all the cash I had earned in the last week. I had to wait till the rush hour was over and made my way to Watford General. The receptionist gave me the directions for the ICU (Intensive Care Unit) which meant it was something serious.

It took me a while to check all the names written outside each room till I found the right one. She was sitting on her bed and when she saw me her face lit up, obviously being glad that I came. She began crying and saying that she realised that she really had nobody to help her in difficult times like this. I felt sorry for her and didn't ask what was wrong with her at this stage. She gave me a list where to look for the items she needed. She signed the handwritten statement that would exonerate me from any liabilities whilst being in her house. I wanted to finish the task as quickly as possible and thus left immediately. There wasn't much traffic and in no time, I was at the house, collected the things for Barbara and drove back to the hospital. Barbara thanked me and went for her purse and had a wad of £ 20 notes in her hand and wanted to put them into my pocket. I gave the money back to her by saying that one day a similar thing could happen to me. After asking what was actually wrong with her, she said that it had something to do with her nerves and she was waiting for a proper diagnosis. We chatted a bit and she thanked me again for the red rose and some fruit I bought her on the way from St Albans. I told her that she could ring me later on and tell me more about her health problem.

It was late in the afternoon when I finally arrived back home, parked my car, collected Duke and took him to the park. I was really tired and after dinner went straight to bed. I rang Barbara and wished her a good night and wasn't ready for any lengthy conversation. Early next morning I was ready for a busy day in France. The group of the three BBC crew were well disciplined. We stopped once before reaching the Folkestone Eurotunnel terminal. I didn't need to use my GPS except for finding the refugee makeshift camp. I suggested that they follow my plan in case of any emergency. By then I already knew that some of the refugees could be hostile towards anybody filming them. I chose a few points where we could meet again. We synchronised our watches and decided they would ring me every twenty minutes to tell me that everything was ok. They appreciated my plans and were commenting and asking, how it was that I was so organised and precise in my planning. I told them that I was an ex tour guide and had remembered a few things about travel planning. I warned them to stick to our B plan to the letter. It all went well on the first evening. We chatted a bit and they were really tense. They confirmed my fears that although they had instructions from their superiors, the reality was of course different.

On the next morning I decided to scale down the meeting points to only two. In any event they would have to run only for some a hundred yards to reach me. I also told them to leave any valuables in my car as at least they would be safe with me. Deep down I wondered how the BBC could even consider sending those three young journalists to such a hot spot untrained, unprepared for any dangerous situation! Barbara rang a few times and I had to tell her not to ring my number till the next day because I needed my line to be free and ready for any calls from the crew.

By 6pm the next day, they finished with what they were doing, and it was 2am when we reached the studios in Wood Lane W12. My poor neighbours and Duke were anxiously waiting for me. I gave my neighbours a small present and £30 which they turned down stating that I paid them well anyway, but I still left the money on their table. Coming indoors the phone was ringing and my answering machine cut in. It was Barbara and a host of other messages. I rang Barbara back straight away and she told me that she was back home again. She was pleased to hear my voice again but she wouldn't tell me what her diagnosis was except that she thought that it was nothing serious and that she would be back at work on the following Monday. She thanked me again and I said that she should stop thanking me all the time. As far as I was concerned a good deed was done and I didn't want to hear about it again. Another few months passed and my love-hate relationship with Barbara still continued, although we weren't intimate as yet.

Russ Abbott, the comedian, was booked for the whole morning. He had to be taken to different studios. We ended up at Teddington studios. Russ told me to go and have lunch since he would be there for a few hours. I wondered if there was enough time to go and see Julia. When she opened her door, she was very surprised to see me again. She invited me indoors and offered a cup of tea. We sat down and she asked me what the reason was for us splitting up. She wanted to have straight answers. I went on telling her that there were never any promises made by me that we would stay together for ever. I mentioned that the distance was a big obstacle since the majority of my work was around west, central and north

London. I had a few customers in Buckinghamshire and other northern counties. She didn't have a driving licence and it took me a while to show her on the road map the distance I had to make to come and see her more often. I also mentioned Duke and her dislike of dogs in general. I also wanted to ask her, what she knew about me and my past life in general but decided not to. All she knew was about my two failed marriages and what she didn't know was the fact that I almost lost my life on more than eight occasions many years prior. I saw no point in telling her how and where. I apologised to Julia that I wasn't ready to settle down. We said our goodbyes and I went back to the studios to take Mr Abbott home.

It was a good day's work and I was glad to head home to be with Duke. Once indoors I noticed my answering machine's lights were flashing. My mail box showed many messages and one of them was from the office. The itinerary was a bit confusing and I had to call the office to get some more information. It showed a passenger's phone number which was that of Clive James. He almost always requested that I be his driver. He lived near Tower Bridge, south of the Thames. I always enjoyed being his driver. Here we go again, me bragging. For my car insurance purposes, I invested in the course for Advanced Motorists and gained a certificate of 'I.A.M.' It is one thing driving yourself or your friends around the UK or London, and there is another thing driving people who probably have their own chauffeur driven limousine. The drive had to be pleasant, not jerky but at the same time making good progress on busy and clogged up London roads. Even then I avoided using the hand-held mobile and used the hands free instead. Clive was on time as usual and I tuned my radio to Classic FM. He never moaned even when we got stuck in heavy traffic because he was aware that I knew all the roads without using a GPS and was doing my best to get him to W11 as quickly as possible.

The next job was to take Lulu, the singer, from her Chelsea pad to the TV studios on Wood Lane. She was very cheerful and laughed at my remarks about how I used to dance to her songs. Being part of the BBC I was able to park on their premises without charge. Their restaurant was described as being dull and with a very unpopular menu, however it suited me personally and was good value for money.

After checking my two phones the third phone's light was flashing, indicating there was a fax. It read to go to the main reception area and take an American to the BBC radio section in Aldwych right in the centre of London. He was already waiting for me. After introducing myself I showed him the way to my car. It was a hot day and he demanded that the air conditioning be switched on immediately. His voice appeared more like a command than just a suggestion. Luckily, very rarely were people as abrupt as him and that was just the beginning. As usual, I wanted to confirm his destination since customers often changed their destination. If there was a difference in the mileage the passengers had to sign for the change of route. If it was only a minor re-route I didn't bother to make any changes to my daily sheet. He suddenly came out with a barrage of insulting words such as: "Don't you know London? Don't you know who I am?"

I didn't know what to say and was speechless. Had I not already been on the main road, I'd have stopped the car and asked my office to send another driver to complete the job instead of me. The only option that was left to me was to ring my office and ask any of the dispatchers to have a listen to his verbal insults but I had to make it so that he wasn't aware that the phone line was still an open call. I asked him again to confirm his destination. He barked in his American accent something like: BBC Bush House. I thanked him and mentally charted the shortest route to Aldwych.

I began to smell cigar smoke coming from the rear seat. I politely asked him not to smoke as it was a non-smoking car. After a few hundred yards the heavy smoke was filling the whole cabin and I slowed down and eventually stopped on the side of a busy Marylebone road. I turned around in my seat and politely told him that it was a non-smoking car and that I was willing to stop somewhere on the next side road where he could step outside and finish his cigar. I added that there would be no extra charge for doing so. I knew that my dispatcher was still on the line. He then started to bang with his hand on the middle console and demanded to drive on and repeating that I didn't know who he was. I just wouldn't move, expecting him to leave my car but instead he put his foot on the air vent in the middle of the console. The damage could be considerable and I asked him not to have his foot on that fragile and expensive console with various switches including the built- in little fridge. He carried on puffing his smoke straight into my face. Of course, all sorts of things went through my mind and I was at the end of my tether but had to stay calm. I opened all the windows because the cigar smoke would linger on for weeks afterwards. I even offered him another option. At the time, I was a non-smoker, but always had a packet of cigarettes in the gloves compartment and suggested that he could have one of the cigarettes instead of his cigar.

He would have none of that, and instead leaned forward and wanted to fiddle with my radio. One of the female dispatchers voice came through my phone, commented how somebody of that repute could behave in such a callous way. She was surprised that I didn't have the name of my passenger. I obviously didn't know that my passenger was assistant to a well- known American congressman, whose name I can't for legal purposes disclose, but he was Donald Rumsfeld's assistant. I had a digital recorder but didn't dare to tape an American politician. It would probably be a 'head-line' in the next day's papers. I had to preserve my dignity and carry on with the 'negotiation' and began to cough without pretending to. I turned into the side road, stopped and stepped out of my car to get some fresh air. In reality I was expecting that he would finally realise that his behaviour was unacceptable.

He decided to get out of the car as well and I was expecting some kind of altercation. What he did next really surprised me. He changed the tone of his voice and asked me if the car was mine and I confirmed that it was. He then began to apologise profusely and said that he thought that I was only a silly part time driver who didn't know London at all. I asked, what made him think so low of me and hadn't he noticed my expensive suit, clean white shirt and that I was wearing a bow tie, an attire just to look as professional as possible? Wasn't my manner good enough for him? I just couldn't help asking him if he behaved without any respect towards all the cab drivers. He must have realised that he could have been secretly taped. He threw half of his huge cigar into the gully and asked me to continue towards Aldwych. I opened all the windows to get rid of the cigar smoke completely. He didn't say a word throughout the rest of the journey.

My office rang me back to enquire how we were progressing and told me that the Aldwych studio would ring me shortly to calculate the time of our arrival. The following call came from Barbara and, I had to tell her to wait for my call. The studio came through straight after that and wanted to know my exact position in order to ascertain if the interview with the American was to be postponed. The interviewer asked, how well I knew the area, to which I replied that he should ask Clive James and Mr Paxman and added that I wasn't being sarcastic. Jeremy Paxman was at that time renowned for his tough style of interviewing, hence his nickname: "The rottweiler!" On one occasion, I did mention to him, how nervous his guests were and how they often asked me, while driving towards studios, if he was really tough on his questions. He replied: "Good, and so they should be."

The interviewer, whom I drove many times before, then mentioned something about my communication problems with my passenger, but I decided to draw the line under the incident and simply said that he most probably mistook me for another, my lookalike driver who he probably had had a run in with. I knew that there were a host of other more important things to worry about and to concentrate on, besides the incident a short while ago with the American. I rang my booking office and told them in a few words that a small problem didn't exist any longer and that we should just forget about the whole thing.

Shortly after we arrived at our destination he politely asked me if I was prepared to wait for him until he finished his interview. It was the BBC policy to accommodate the VIP guests' wishes. I had to ring my office again and requested the change of my work schedule. It was approved and I even had enough time to give Barbara a call. She had apparently left the hospital and was preparing an evening meal and wondered if I was prepared to come to her place and have dinner with her. I paused for a while and confirmed that I would come but only if Duke could join me, which she agreed.

After a while, the studio asked me to come to the front entrance and take him to another BBC studio in Upper Regents Street. They also told me that they had informed my office of changes and added mileage. According to my calculation my day would be good in respect of my projected earnings. That part of London was always congested and a chance of finding a parking space was nil, therefore I quickly stopped at the 'Prêt à Manger' and grabbed a quick snack and returned to the side entrance of Regents Street studios.

I spotted a few paparazzi at the main entrance and that prompted me to change the spot where I should wait for him to appear again. I rang the studio and told them of my decision and advised them to send my passenger to the rear entrance. They thanked me for that and listened to my advice. The BBC policy was always: Never pick up any passengers whereby they would have to endure the walk through the gauntlet of photographers and the autograph seekers, but always look for a back entrance to be the pick-up point.

Mr Tony Benn and most of the VIPs who I drove, were pleased with my in-depth knowledge of London and my technique of avoiding the crowds and the paparazzi. Shortly after I joined the BBC back in 1994, I for the very first time encountered the real paparazzi and had very soon learned how they operate. Some of them would come to my car and offer a cash incentive for any information about my passengers and to reveal their phone numbers and home addresses. Again, their offers didn't work with me. The Ivy restaurant was one of their top spots to ply their business.

The American finally came out after nearly 3 hours wait and I told him to quickly board the car. As we drove off there were already some people running from the main entrance to the side entrance where I had waited, but luckily, they were too late. He was by then a completely changed man, by seeing people running after us with their cameras at the ready. He wanted to go back to his hotel in George Street, to the Churchill Hotel to be more precise. He then asked for my boss's name and I indicated that I had no boss as such and had my PCO certificate issued to me personally and that I was a subcontractor to a few cab firms but mainly did the work for the BBC. As he was stepping out of the car, he asked if I still felt offended. I said that I wasn't offended but sad and that little incident was already forgotten. He produced a $20 Dollar bill and left it on the dashboard. "I will ask for you if I have to give another interview in the next two days left of my stay in the UK." As soon as he shut the rear door, I rang my office and told them to forget about the whole episode with my passenger. The office supervisor also came on-line, and commented how I had just 'earned the nick name 'Zinco, the diplomat!'

It was time to go back home and collect Duke and make my way towards St Albans. Barbara greeted me as if we had known each other for ages. Duke went quiet and didn't like her and even growled when Barbara wanted to stroke him. It was a surprise to me since he had never done this before. Was it in some way a warning? I let him out into Barbara's huge back garden where he had a good run. He even chased some of the squirrels. At least he had some fun.

Barbara was preparing a leg of lamb in Greek style. Even Duke knew that he would soon have his dinner. I asked Barbara if there was a lot of garlic in the gravy because garlic is one of the vegetables that would cause havoc with Duke's intestines and could be fatal. After all he only weighed some 7lbs and could be unwell in a very short time. Barbara asked how I would like the potatoes to be cooked. I like them to be crusty and brown. The Yorkshire pudding was almost ready and I helped Barbara to lay the table. The kitchen was very clean and so were the plates and glasses. I was getting really hungry and couldn't wait to tuck into that crispy leg of lamb. It tasted heavenly and superb. Drinking of any sort of alcohol was out of the question because after dinner I was to drive back home. Some 8 years before, I nearly lost my licence because I hadn't allowed enough time for the alcohol to be digested. It was a mistake made in the wake of my mother's death. The police officer who stopped and breathalysed me didn't use the breathalysing kit properly and I was let off.

Barbara was born in London but she and her family moved to Borehamwood, Hertfordshire. Both of her parents were of Irish origin. It is very important that I categorically don't intend to show any disrespect to the Irish community, wherever in the world they are, in all the following chapters. It just happened that Barbara was of Irish descent. It is also important that whatever happened between Barbara and me, has nothing to do with the BBC Corporation in general. It just happened that Barbara was an BBC employee.

It was getting late and I announced that it was time for Duke and me to head home. She kept saying that we could stay overnight at her place in her son's room. I wouldn't have it as the next morning I had an early job. It looked like it was a busy time for me the next day. If I stayed I would still have to leave her house early the next morning. It meant that I would have to leave at 5am in order to get Duke home and then drive to Gatwick airport, pick up my passenger and then continue wherever my passenger wished to go. She understood and asked me if I would accept an invitation to a dinner on another occasion. I promised that I would.

Duke slept throughout the journey back to London. I wanted to go straight to bed but the answering machine was bleeping and showed that the messaging folder was full. There were dozens of messages. My office message was the last one. Apparently, they tried to contact me throughout the evening. I checked my Nokia handset and discovered that that message box was full as well. I rang my office to find out whether there was something urgent to deal with.

The dispatcher wanted to change my plans for the next day. I was to present myself at the MOD (Ministry of Defence) in London, SW1 at noon and take some of the officials to the BBC Bush House in the Strand and wait for them and afterwards take them to Farnborough. They would attend the Air Show of the year. I quite liked the itinerary and accepted it. I would probably have a chance to look at some of the latest military planes and the rest.

I was glad that my itinerary was changed and there was no early start.

I was on time and approached the MOD building where my passengers were already waiting for me. There had been a misunderstanding about the pickup time. I showed the BBC researcher my portable digital fax document proving that as far as I was concerned, I was on time. It immediately defused the situation. Unbeknown to me, the passengers were a group of American military personnel and didn't make any fuss and after their interview was over, without any further ado, we were on our way towards Farnborough. They began to talk about their plans and were asking me if my car was equipped with some kind of recording devices, because they noticed two microphones situated above the windscreen. I assured them that those little gadgets were factory fitted microphones for my hands-free phone and I suggested that I could tune into the Classic FM, if that would keep them happy. They agreed. Of course there was a digital recorder in my top jacket pocket but I have never taped any of my passengers' conversations. It's not and it wasn't my nature to record anything, other than using it in a possible car accident. When my passengers wanted to change the route or extend their journey, pickup an extra passenger or there was a danger of being accused of not handing back items, which were left behind, I would call my controllers and let the passengers talk to them. I nearly had to use that recorder on two occasions, as in the case of what happened with Barbara and that American congressman.

PLEASE, LET ME MAKE IT CLEAR, THE BBC HAD NEVER ASKED ME TO RECORD ANY OF THE

PASSENGERS' CONVERSATION WHATSOEVER! If their own fleet of cars had any listening devices fitted, I certainly didn't know. In those days the dash cams were very expensive and in the case of an accident I just wanted to have some kind of back up. I also had a digital camera in my glove compartment which was also for the protection of my interests and again in case of an accident. I have never asked any of my passengers to allow me to take their photo, neither have I taken any photos of my passengers without them knowing. Now, come to think of it, I wish that there were some photos taken and saved for my personal album.

As usual we arrived safely at Farnborough and my passengers were taken care of by another American official. My passengers wanted me to wait for them as long as it would take and bring them back to their London Churchill Hotel. I was shown the way to the restaurant where I could have my lunch and the exact spot where my passengers would be in a few hours time. I gave them my phone number just in case there were some changes in their plans but in any event, I would always be close to my car. It was very interesting to see all the planes taking off and landing. It brought back the memories of my own flying experience 4 years before when I gained my PPL (Private Pilots' Licence).There was so much to see that it would take more than a whole day to take all that experience in.

That day every so often Barbara kept ringing me. She wanted to know if I was still seeing Julia and when I would come to dinner at her place again. I felt awkward and tried to avoid any of her questioning. Deep inside I felt that one day we would end up in bed together, since there was nothing negative in her physical appearance.

Shaun, one of her previous drivers, warned me that I should keep away from her and if I ever went to bed with her, her son might join us. I asked him what made him say that. He went on to say that he drove one of her previous boyfriends and that his name was Dave and that he could give me his phone number so that I would have 'first- hand information' about Barbara. "Zinco, I must warn you again, to not get involved with Barbara, since her son might join you and share the bed. Ring up Dave and talk to him and you'll save yourself a lot of trouble." Dave was one of the top cameramen at BBC. My immediate reaction, to what Shaun told me was, that he probably wanted to date Barbara and was saying all those things out of jealousy, but I nevertheless took Dave's phone number. I listened to my instinct and wasn't going to ring him at all. I had no right to further enquire about Barbara behind her back and had put the subject on the 'back burner' and waited for her to ring me instead.

When she rang again I accepted her invitation but with one condition, that I would pay for whatever she would need to prepare the dinner. I didn't know that she was on sick leave for a couple of days. We arranged that I would come to St Albans in the coming week. I wanted to wait for a job which would take me to or near St Albans on that day, thus saving on petrol. There were a lot of BBC employees living in that area and it wasn't difficult to ask my despatcher to allocate any of the jobs booked for that direction. He even cracked a joke by saying that I was probably succumbing to Barbara's advances. I felt embarrassed and didn't comment any further.

On the following day, the auction house in Salem Road, West London W2 left a message that they had a few lots that weren't sold and not collected by the vendors and would I be interested to give them an offer. Obviously, they might have contacted other shop keepers and probably the lots were not of any great value. I took a chance and went to see what was on offer. There were boxes and boxes of old clock mechanisms, springs, loose clogs and clock housings, and I could tell that some of them were well over a century old. The price was so silly that I bought them straight away. It cost me £60 and I just couldn't believe that those lots weren't sold. I went home to collect my jeep and at the same time cancelled any work for that day. The office wasn't very pleased with my cancelling, but I knew that the lots just bought would bring me hundreds of pounds.

Barbara was ringing me every hour to ask me how I was getting on. She gave me the list of what she would need to cook the dinner and asked again if I really wanted to pay for all of it. To pay for the ingredients was nothing to me considering how much I was earning. I just wanted to have fair play. My neighbours were prepared to look after Duke for the next day.

I bought a double portion of smoked salmon at the famous Brick Lane Bagel shop just for Duke. The next stop was 'Marks and Sparks' in Finchley, North London. It was getting dark and I called Barbara to say that I was on my way and would be there in about ten minutes or so. She sounded worried and I wanted to know what was worrying her, but she didn't want to say. I thought that she would probably tell me when I arrived.

As I approached her house the windows were wide open and

there was smoke billowing out of the living room. I jumped out of the car and rushed through the front door. The smoke was coming out of the kitchen and to be precise out of the oven. I asked her why on earth she didn't tell me that the leg of lamb was just about to burst in flames and why hadn't she called the fire brigade? I grabbed a blanket from the living room, removed the baking dish from the oven and covered it with the blanket and threw the still smouldering, charred meat and the dish through the window. I then filled a large pot with water and doused the hob and the smoking oven. Already, there were neighbours standing across the street, asking if they should ring the fire brigade. I calmed them down and said that all was under control. We left the door and windows open and sat down in the living room.

After a while she admitted that she wanted to go to a local Waitrose to buy some wine and whilst she was there she had a coffee and just forgot that the leg of lamb was in the oven. I decided to stay for a while till the house was properly aired and then I would make my way back to London. At the back of my mind was the question: Was she on some kind of strong medication or drugs? My manners would not allow me to ask her any further questions. All I wanted was a strong cup of tea and a biscuit. Barbara wanted to cook again but I politely told her not to bother since it was already past midnight and the dinner wouldn't be ready for the next 2 hours at the earliest. She was in tears when I prepared to leave. In my opinion, she was in no state to cook another meal. I stayed for the next hour and tried to calm her down. She rang her son Andrew in Durham and told him about how my quick thinking and action had stopped the fire spreading through the kitchen and possibly through the rest of the house. I made sure that the back door was closed and locked and suggested that she leave the upper floor windows open till the morning.

At about 1.30am I was on my way home. I was in a sense glad to be out of that house. Deep inside my gut was telling me not to go back to that place again. A BAD OMEN! Whilst driving, I was thinking how to avoid any further contact with Barbara. But how? She apparently persuaded some 8 of her co-workers to be driven by our BBC Company. If I decided to stop driving Barbara, her colleagues would probably join a different company and I would be blamed. I would then in the process lose a bit of my preferential treatment. I didn't know what to do. All I knew was that I had to distance myself from Barbara and do it quick! My neighbours were still not in bed and Duke was going mad to see me. I was hungry and tired. I made sure that the phones were switched off completely so that nobody could disturb my sleep.

Duke woke me up at 9am and wanted to go out. We went for a quick walk without a phone on me. Barbara was constantly on my mind. How to avoid her and her constant ringing? Above all, what was she expecting from me? After all she earned well at the corporation, hence she was able, in my opinion, to meet the mortgage payments.

When we came back from the little park I could hear the phone ringing as I stepped into the hallway. It was the office and the dispatcher wanted to know, if I would be available to do some work on the following Sunday. It would be a well paid job. Sunday was my trading day in Brick Lane and I had to turn down the job. I wanted to keep my shop going in case my job would come to an end for whatever reason. The dispatcher wasn't very pleased and since he was new, he didn't know my arrangements with his boss, that on Sundays I was in my shop. He then offered me a journey to Brighton with one of David Dimbleby's associates from Barnes, just a mile from Hammersmith, South London. It was a good earner. I would be paid to drive to Brighton, wait for a few hours and then bring the passenger safely back to Barnes.

It was Saturday and there was hardly any traffic on the road. Upon our arrival, Mr Dimbleby offered me a cup of tea. I declined his offer by saying that I would have a lunch and would be close to his house in case his guest would like to return back to London sooner than planned. There was a convenience shop nearby and I bought something to eat. The phone rang very soon after and it was Barbara.

She began to apologise about the previous night. I decided to listen to her for as long as she wanted and maybe she would reveal more about herself. She was explaining the sequence of events on the previous night and how forgetful she sometimes was. She was on the phone for more than half an hour and was telling me about her failed marriage to a man from Corfu. She had lived there for nearly two years and returned back to UK. According to her she was badly treated by her husband's family. She managed to bring her son Andrew back with her to UK. She had studied journalism in London some fourteen years before and was accepted by the corporation to work in the satellite section. She furthered her career quite rapidly and was promoted to a cost accessor, dealing mainly with the European Broadcasting Union. She repeated exactly what her well paid job entailed. It was to give prices for the satellite feeds of news and various programs and sell them to other corporations and TV stations around the world. I jokingly commented that one day she might forget that one of the satellites was on fire. On my question of her health in general she didn't want to comment and promised she would one day tell me. She forgot that I had bought the steaks and all the trimmings to be cooked upon my arrival, so I didn't say a word about it.

Mr Dimbleby's guest was ready to leave and we were lucky that there was only light traffic on the way back. It was 7pm when we reached Barnes. After Duke was collected and we had our dinner Barbara was on the line again. I wasn't in the mood to talk for too long and wanted to have some rest before a busy day ahead in the shop. Duke woke me up at 2am and was already at the front door. He knew that he would be able to run freely along the shops and stalls in Brick Lane. The Lane was closed to traffic on Sundays and there was no danger of him being run over.

At 6am I went to get some breakfast for Duke and Arnold, my neighbour who helped with my crystals deal in Kensington. He was very fond of my pet Duke and so was his daughter. Obviously only the best would do for Duke and Arnold's breakfasts. Bagels filled with a double portion of smoked salmon. Before I knew it the street came to life. There were people waiting for me to open the shop. Most of them wanted to buy my crystals. There were hundreds of other items displayed inside. Arnold came to see how the trade was going. He had a lucrative business himself in the yard almost opposite my shop. He admired the way I handled the customers. Then, out of nowhere Barbara appeared and sat herself down and calmly said that she wanted to help me out.

After seeing all the people milling around my two huge stalls outside the shop, she got up and said that she was serious about her offer and I paused for a moment and agreed. She wanted to know what was to be done. I said that the most important thing was to watch that items were not stolen-pilfered whilst my eyes were on taking the money and giving change. Deep inside my head was the question why was Barbara coming to see me. "Let's see how it goes" was my thought and brushed aside any suspicion. After all there was nothing remotely illegal about my life and business. In fact, she came to be quite handy since I was on my own till the arrival of my two helpers. She asked if she should go and get some tea from the bagel shop some two hundred yards away and didn't want me to pay for it.

Arnold came over to me as she went down the lane and asked who was that attractive lady, to which I replied that it was my new girlfriend and nearly bit my lip by telling such a lie. But then again it dawned on me that she probably wanted to be my girlfriend after all. There was a wave of new customers heading for my shop and an outside enormous stall laden with mainly chandelier cut glass bits. As usual I never took any banknotes out of my pocket, merely not to look flashy. Barbara was good at dealing with the customers. I took her quickly inside the shop and told her that she should not price any of the items and that it would be explained to her later. I knew most of the customers and treated each one of them differently. For example, my prices to any trader would be lower so to let them also make a living. 'What goes around, comes around.' Barbara took all that on board and did everything the way I wanted. My pockets were full of bank notes and I was very

pleased with my takings so far. At any moment I was expecting Gary or Joe to arrive. They at least had money to make me another offer for the crystals. In the last months alone, according to my calculations, I must have bagged over £15000 and thought, if the things go the way they have, I might be able to buy another car. My limo was over four years old and it would be nice to buy another brand new Mercedes limousine. I could part exchange my old one and the clients would love it!

Being as stubborn as usual, I was going to go against my accountant's advice not to buy and pay outright for a new car. I wanted to buy it in one go because of the worry in case of any illness, when the instalments would not be met.

The trade eased a bit and we sat down with Duke beside me and sipped our tea. Barbara looked quite happy being in my company and commented about my tan. There was a chance to strike up a conversation and the possibility to change my decision to cut any ties with her. She appeared to be a bit evasive with her words with regards to questions about her health. The change of subject led our conversation to the subject of her son.

Like most mothers she spoke highly of him. Barbara did everything to get her son as far as she was able to go to the University of Durham in the north of England. She was complaining about her ex- husband and how he didn't bother to come and see him during his stay at Durham Uni. Being married twice and engaged a few times more myself, I knew that it normally takes 'two to tango.' We went on to talk about her work at the BBC. She had a few problems with some of her working colleagues. It appeared that there was a lot of jealousy involved between her

and her co-workers. She knew her job down to the last detail. We all know that it's quite common that sometimes co-workers can display and manifest some sort of envy.

The time flew by fast and I started to pack up. It took me an hour before all the stuff was put back into the shop. I politely told her that I would take her to Kings Cross station from where she could get a direct train to St Albans. Maybe she wanted to come with me and stay overnight at my place, but I told her that my flat was in a bit of disarray, thus indicating that I wasn't ready to forge some kind of relationship. After two failed marriages and a few engagements I was determined to give myself a lot of time before committing myself to another serious relationship. I might sound too picky but that was not true.

None of my partners in the past had any interest in going to the theatre, neither had they any liking for classical music. After all I had spent countless hours learning and practising on pianos throughout my life. I longed to go with my partner to any of the concerts and immerse myself in the sounds of either a solo pianist, performing artists, or the orchestra.

This time round, I just wished to meet a partner with similar interests. Barbara, from what I gathered during the conversation, also had no time for any sort of classical music. Throughout the journey towards Kings Cross station, Duke simply didn't want to sit next to her, whereas he was friendly with almost anybody. Was this a warning of some sort? We had arrived at Kings Cross station and I offered Barbara the money for the rail fare, but she declined the offer. She also wouldn't accept any money for her help in the shop. She just said that I was very tactful with my customers and

would like to come again on the following Sunday. I agreed but on the proviso that she be paid for doing so.

There was hardly any traffic on my way home. After checking my fax machine to see if there were any messages I went to bed. Within 10 minutes Barbara rang, and wanted to know if she could entice me to a cooked meal the following week. My reply was yes and I wished her a good night. Due to my tiredness, I didn't even check how much money was in my pockets. It was 7am when the phone rang. It was my office. There was a job offer to go to Manchester where there would be a passenger by the name of Mark Thompson waiting for me to take him back to the BBC London studios and I should be there by 4pm.

Mr Thompson was the new BBC Director General who took over from Greg Dyke. By 8am I was on my way. After a few hours into the journey, Barbara rang and enquired how I was progressing. It was strange that she had all the details of my job. It just sounded a bit spooky, her knowledge about the trip which had nothing to do with her department. I decided not to challenge her as to how she got the information about my job. She seemed to be in a good mood. In those days, it was still not considered to be a serious offence using a mobile phone whilst driving and we chatted for a while. Again, she dodged any questions about her health. Knowing the BBC policies regarding any health issues reasonably well, I assumed that she probably suffered from some kind of ailment which wasn't life threatening. I finished off my conversation with a promise to call her when I reached Manchester.

Mr Thompson was ready to go back to London so we set off immediately. The motorways weren't busy and we covered the

first 150 miles in good time. My passenger wasn't saying much and I preferred it that way in order to concentrate on my driving. Some 50 miles from London he woke up and asked how long to go before we reached our destination. According to my estimation it would take another hour. He commented about my driving and complimented me on my cool way of handling all the situations, regarding other driver's stupid actions.

The only thing left once reaching home was to feed Duke, check for any unanswered calls and find out if there were any letters to take care of. As usual, my pet Duke was collected from my neighbour and I gave them £20. They always tried to refuse any money for minding my dog. I still think that I was very lucky to have such good neighbours. Duke also got used to them having him around while I was at work. Back indoors the phone was already ringing. Barbara just wanted to know if I was safely back home.

Whilst I was on the phone, Duke began to growl the moment he heard her voice. After finishing talking to Barbara there was something sinister about Duke's barking. Was Duke telling me something? Come to think of it, he was, as it transpired a few weeks later! I checked my messages left on the answer phone, while Duke had his favourite meal of braised salmon. There was a job lined up for me for the next day to go and to pick-up Mrs Esther Rantzen from her home in Hampstead and take her to the BBC studios in Upper Regents Street and to wait for her and take her to the Wood Lane studios. It was a nice little job. She was and I hope still is very professional. I could tell that she knew inner and outer London streets and roads very well. Some of the other drivers have described her as her being "obnoxious." I found her to be very polite. I presume this was partly down to my near perfect knowledge of London as well.

According to my experience, I divided the celebrities and my passengers in two groups. In the first group were well-known public figures (actors, actresses, film stars, like Peter Fonda for example, broadcasters, producers, film directors) who would in general 'shy away from public exposure and would fall into the first of my groups. I also discovered that more often than not, celebrities of a 'high calibre' were more tolerant and more understanding, if I was late for various reasons.

The second group consisted of those lesser known personalities. They tried to give us a hard time regarding waiting time. I despised those passengers, but sometimes I had to accept the "rough" with the "smooth" and help the company out, since nobody else on that day wanted to drive those 'snow flakes.' It mostly happened with the airport pick- up jobs and would begin when a passenger would spot me straight away. They would then wander around the arrival hall, 'fishing for compliments' and finally, after parading (I used to say 'loitering') around for some twenty minutes or more and after nobody asked them for their autograph, would ring my number and ask where on earth I was! Regardless whether I knew who the passenger was, I couldn't just run after them calling out their name, because their journey might have been booked with another company at the last moment. And then the real joke begins, by them denying ever seeing me, refusing to sign for the waiting time, including parking fees.

The job would be priced at, let's say £40. The petrol alone to go to Heathrow, driving the passenger back to Hampstead and then driving back to or near BBC studios, would come to £18-20 pounds. The parking would come to £10-12 and after spending three hours on the job, I would have earned £8 pounds which wouldn't keep me in business for long.

Mrs Rantzen fell into the first category and I had never seen her as an attention seeker. I remember once driving her from the BBC Millbank studios towards Upper Regent Street studios. The traffic coming from Hyde Park corner going north was really heavy. Near the Marble Arch roundabout, I swiftly turned down the slope towards the Hyde Park underground car park, past the main entrance and came out at the traffic lights which were showing green saving her considerable time. She seemed to be impressed and whenever I drove her around London, she was always pleasant.

Ms Kirsty Wark, the Newsnight presenter, equally never wanted to wander around the arrival halls. On the contrary, she used to wait next to the 'Coca-Cola fridge' outside the terminal 1 building, in order to save her time. She was, and hope still is, a very professional lady.

Occasionally, I would privy to a sad scene. A well- known TV personality wanted to be taken from Broadcasting House in Upper Regent Street back home in Battersea. She would normally be picked up at the rear entrance. On that day she decided to leave through the front entrance, and I was going to walk her back towards the rear entrance, as at the front of Broadcasting House were double yellow lines. There were dozens of autograph chasers and a few photographers. I felt sorry for that lady, because I knew, whom the crowd was waiting for. Sadly, they weren't waiting for her, but for another, much younger upcoming celebrity! At the end of the journey, she managed to sound cheerful and all she said was: "Once upon a time, the crowds were waiting for me."

I continued my way towards Baker Street to pick up a very placid and punctual broadcaster, John Suchet, who worked for ITV and Sky, and to my horror realised that he was actually waiting for me at the Sky studios in Isleworth-west from London. Due to my punctuality in the past, he made no fuss whatsoever.

Barbara was ringing me constantly throughout that afternoon, but I was too busy to pick up the phone. When the working day was over I rang her and asked her not to constantly ring me and that her ringing was distracting me and my passengers. She apologised and added that she only wanted to know if I would like to take her home but since I didn't answer her call, she booked someone else.

Obviously I would have been paid by the corporation but still asked her to use the SMS services in the future if she wanted to contact me. It worked! From then on, the phone calls from her stopped for a while. Something just didn't add up with the story she was telling me, about booking and driving with someone else. The following Sunday she turned up unannounced at my shop in Brick Lane again and this time she came early.

I had two guys helping me, on and off, to put up the stall outside the shop and bringing out some heavy boxes from the basement. I paid them well and wanted them to stay with me on a regular basis in the future and throughout that day. It took the pressure off me watching the stall and the shop on my own. They would go to get breakfast for themselves, for Arnold, Duke and Barbara from the same bagel shop. The two helpers were thankful that I treated them to a breakfast. I earned enough cash to meet those breakfast costs over and over again.

Barbara was fascinated with my usual display of the outside stall including chandelier crystal bits. I just wanted to give myself more time to think if we could be an item. She was quite a bit taller than me and very attractive. Deep inside I only wished that she hadn't been so rude and inconsiderate on that evening when we first met. I also wondered, why she was so persistent to be in my company, whereas she could meet someone at her work place or any other place for that matter. At the end of the day, I was only a second-hand shop leaseholder with two flats above the shop. Surely, she could find someone more compatible than me. At the end of the busy trading day I took her to King's Cross station. Barbara declined again to be paid for the work she did at the shop. She asked if she could at a later date come to my place. I promised that one day I would cook something for her when she came.

Due to getting up at all hours, the tiredness slowly got hold of me. I began to realise that for over a year I had been working seven days a week and had none or very little time to relax and this had to change and had to change soon. I decided to go to one of the theatres in Drury Lane as soon as practically possible. Barbara would be invited to join me if she wanted. It would also give me an opportunity to invite Barbara back to my place. She would be on my territory and I would finally be able to talk to her freely, of course in an unobtrusive way.

There were a lot of messages left on my answering machine. They were all related to my work. There were two well paid jobs allocated to me for the next day. Jill Dando had to be driven to her fiancés' residence in Chiswick West London and then on to

Gatwick Airport. This journey was booked and subsequently cancelled, through the company, whose controllers were often negligent with Jill's details of destination, explained in one of the following chapters. A while later I would drive Mr Peter Bazalgette, the film producer, from Heathrow airport back to his Notting Hill residence. When on that day Barbara rang, I didn't tell her about my plan and the invitation.

What immediately worried me was the fact that my place had to be cleared of all the clutter and all the unnecessary stuff around my place. All the places I have lived at were always untidy but not dirty. My estimation was that some three hours of hard work would be needed to make my place look neat and cosy. Quite a lot of items had to be taken to my garage. My living room and bedroom had very expensive oriental deep-shag carpets. My upright piano was also an expensive piece of furniture, due to the keys covered with ivory. My china crockery and cutlery were 'fit for any Lady of the manor.' My kitchen was fitted with all the mod-cons. Duke had his own little bed at the bottom of my bed although he would usually curl up at my feet on the bed.

Only one question remained, what to cook? I decided to cook something Slovenian. I made polenta pancakes to go with sautéed potatoes as a side dish. One of the most popular main dishes in Slovenia is a thinly cut-sliced filet of calf which is breaded with real breadcrumbs, dipped in egg yolk and deep fried. It's called a Wiener Schnitzel and since Slovenia was once part of the Austrian Empire, it also became partly a Slovenian national dish. An organic reared chicken soup would obviously be cooked as a starter. An apple strudel would be our pudding. The strudel consisted of freshly grated apples, honey, various spices such as cinnamon, cloves and vanilla essence and baked in layers of filo pastry and was also an Austrian adopted dish. I learned how to bake it from my mother.

I had my plan carefully worked out as regards the dinner and all that was left was to ring a ticketing agent. Luck was on my side and there was a performance at one of the theatres in Drury Lane where Judy Dench was performing as a guest actress the next evening. I had driven her on two occasions and liked her as an actress.

The plan was going just as I wanted. I cancelled all but one of the jobs lined up for the next day. The well- known comedian, whom I also drove a few times, Jimmy Davidson. He requested that I take him to Gatwick airport. He lived in a mansion which used to belong to the actor, Oliver Reed. Jimmy always used to greet me via intercom: "I know it's you Zinco." He was subsequently accused of some sexual misconduct and was in due course cleared of alleged charges. I have witnessed, how he had to make his way back to my car in a hurry, because there were some women chasing him! He didn't have to even think of any misconduct, while there were many women after him.

I would like to take an opportunity to shed light on some of the scenes I saw first-hand at the BBC after some 'rock stars' performances. Multiple times young girls succeeded in finding a way to avoid the security personnel and managed to come closer to 'a rock star' as he was leaving. They would throw their underwear on the bonnets of their cars and even stop in front of cars and literally strip in front of them. Some didn't even appear to be older than 15 at the time! I'm sure there must be tons of security camera tapes lying somewhere in the BBC archives to confirm my observation. I have never witnessed a male fan strip in front of a female rock star!

After a good night's sleep, I was ready to begin preparing our dinner. Obviously a fully pre-cooked dinner wouldn't taste good at all. The hours went by quickly and late in the afternoon I went to Barbara's house to collect her. She was almost ready. She showed me the rest of the house. I had noticed that her two wardrobes were full of expensive clothes and dresses. Her son's room was as untidy as mine often was. Barbara made me a cup of tea and I strolled through her back garden. Duke followed me as usual. The garden shed looked dilapidated and the grass appeared to be dishevelled, a clear sign that Barbara lived alone. Soon she called out of the kitchen window that she was ready to go.

It didn't take us long to reach my place in London and all that was needed was to leave Duke with my neighbours. Barbara waited in the car and it only took a couple of minutes before we were setting off. Barbara asked, where we were actually going. "To the theatre" I replied. I found a parking spot nearby and we entered the entrance hall full of other theatre goers. Barbara looked splendid. We were led to and shown our seats. She was very surprised and bemused. She admitted that she, up to then, had only been to the theatre once in her life. I sincerely hoped that she would like it.

At the end of the performance I gathered that she didn't get the plot. It didn't bother me. It was around 10pm when we arrived at my flat. She was impressed with my décor and various pricey objects of art. She wanted to see my bedroom. I often went to Harrods and Harvey Nicholls sales and the bedroom looked like a show piece. The bed linen and the floral bed spread as well as matching curtains, were of Laura Ashley design. A huge floral deep cut carpet was bought at one of the auction rooms in London and she was very impressed. I added that my aim was not to impress her nor anybody else for that matter. She commented on the cleanliness of my kitchen. I opened a bottle of sparkling wine and filled both of our glasses. She asked me if it would offend me if she didn't drink any alcohol because of the medication she was on. I replied that it didn't bother me in the slightest and went to collect Duke from my neighbour. Duke looked at Barbara and didn't want to greet her, instead he went straight into his basket. Barbara was one of the few people he didn't like despite seeing her a few times already. It really puzzled me. I checked the food in the oven and all that was needed was to deep fry the 'Vienna Schnitzel.'

I was hungry and so was she and we wiped the plates clean. It was her first time eating something Slovenian and she liked it. In no time the table was cleared and the dishes were in the dish washer. I had my second glass of wine and felt satisfied. Barbara asked where I had learned to cook and I told her of my stay in Switzerland. The conversation went on to various subjects but it was my decision not to tell her about my dramatic and traumatic past life. I wanted to know about her life in more details, especially about her health. After a while she opened up a bit more. She revealed that her husband and his family back in Corfu didn't treat her well and because of that she moved back to St Albans with her then very young son. She was working a lot of overtime to support and pay for her son's university and boarding expenses and she worried about not being able to continue to support him until the end of his studies. I wanted to hear more about her last boyfriend and find out why they split up. She already knew about my two marriages and my life as a driving instructor. I wanted to know if she was solely blaming her husband and her past boyfriends and not partly herself. She didn't want to comment on this subject. I changed the tactics and showed her my photo album. She looked at some of the photos more closely. Suddenly one of the photos fell on the floor. I could see that she had difficulty holding anything in her left hand for more than a minute. I asked her if she had a neurological health problem. She had a beautiful face and her lips were slightly twitching before she answered my question. She had a disease called Multiple Sclerosis. I was shaken by the news and subsequently she burst into tears and I tried to console her as best I could. It took her a while to compose herself and she didn't want to talk about her illness any longer.

It was getting really late and I suggested that it was time to go to bed. She must have known by now that we would not drive back to St Albans. I offered her a pair of my pyjamas and said that I would sleep on my chaise longue which was comfortable enough. She insisted that she instead would sleep on my chaise longue but I wouldn't have it. My bathroom was full of fresh towels, bathrobes as well as a new pair of slippers. On the long glass shelf above the bathroom sink was an array of expensive bottles of scented bath oils, Christian Dior, Hermes, Gucci perfumes which were new, unopened and bought at different auction rooms. Of course they were original and were bought not to be sold but to be given as a present to some of my female visitors. There was one question which was, that she never asked me to play something

74

on the piano. It confirmed to me that she wasn't interested in any classical music. It was fine by me, but I was longing to meet a lady, who as mentioned before, had similar interests in life to mine. I went on asking her if she had many friends at her place of work and her reply hardly surprised me when she confessed that there were only two female co-workers who she trusted. I empathised with her since my life long experiences with jealousy and envy at my work-places were all too familiar to me as well. Nevertheless, I managed to ignore the fact that she didn't like the classical piece I played on my piano. I still wanted to know a bit more about her medical condition, bearing in mind that she was my guest and I didn't want to bombard her with too many questions. I think what I wanted to know was whether she was receiving proper treatment regarding her MS. She was beginning to explain her illness in quite some detail. Her explanation tallied with my research which I did on the NHS websites. Barbara was fully aware that she would possibly never reach a very old age and that in the meanwhile the disease would progress with time. My own research also revealed that the main possible trigger was an unknown virus and possibly a stressful life.

I had to interrupt her because there was a message with details of my next job. Bill Turnbull, the breakfast presenter, wanted to be taken from his home in Buckinghamshire to the TV Centre, but I had to turn it down due to my late night drinking. He normally had to be at the studios by 5am. He kept bees and his honey tasted superb.

We continued to talk, but I decided to change the subject. Barbara was getting tired after discussions about her father who was in a home for the elderly in Borehamwood and wanted to go to bed. We said good night and she headed for the bathroom. I closed the door. Duke was already in his basket and I made myself as comfortable as possible on my chaise longue. Not very comfortable to sleep on to say the least.

Duke woke me up and wanted to go for his morning walk. We left very quietly so as not to wake Barbara who was still asleep. Upon our return Barbara was already cooking our breakfast. She found her way around my kitchen and managed to find some eggs and bacon and sausages. As usual my phone was ringing and the controller was letting me know that a nice job was lined up for me in the afternoon. Moira Stuart was to be taken somewhere in central London again. She was quite pleased with me in the past and my presumption was that she requested me to be her driver for that afternoon and evening. It was on her private account and I knew it was something very private. She was invited to a lavish function and it would be a betrayal to Moira to reveal the name of the venue and to divulge her home address. In my mind, she wasn't just a news reader, because we discussed a bit about the 'parallel' universes on few occasions. We used to call her journey a 'wait and return', and those jobs were remunerated handsomely.

Barbara agreed to stay at my place and look after Duke. She wanted to do some shopping and cook our dinner. My only worry was that my dog would try to bite her since he just didn't like her. Just in case I had put a muzzle on Duke's mouth for that afternoon and evening until my return. It was around 9 o'clock when I finally arrived home. Barbara was sitting in the living room and watching TV. There was no smell of any cooking. Barbara got up and wanted to know why the cooker wasn't working. I realised that she must have left the cooker turned on unattended for quite some time and the safety feature switched the cooker off. She was very upset and I suggested that we should have a fish and chips takeaway dinner instead.

About a mile down my road was a well-known fish and chip shop called 'The Seashell.' It is still there today. In no time at all I brought back two huge portions of delightful fillets of cod with all the trimmings. There was a child's portion of fish for Duke as well. Barbara couldn't remember the last time she had such a tasty fish and chips dinner. I would never know the secret of finding all the places to get a perfect meal, without my friend in Brick Lane, Arnold, who said "Zinco, wherever you see a black cab or black cabs, without the driver in it, outside of any restaurant or takeaway shop you can be sure that the food is good!" It's still true to this day.

From my open plan kitchen, I could see Barbara was going through her big shopping bag and laid the garments she had bought on the sofa. She had bought herself a complete, new outfit. From the blouse, to the underwear and shoes. She planned to stay another night which was some kind of sign that she was comfortable staying another night with me. She was planning to go back to work the next day. I called my dispatcher and booked the job for Barbara from London W2 to the BBC in Wood Lane-Shepherds Bush. I could invoice the BBC for the whole journey from St Albans to Wood Lane, but decided not to, as my earnings were good enough and there was no need to cheat the Corporation which treated me so honourably.

There was some wine left from the previous night and again

Barbara wouldn't drink it. She sat opposite me and showed me her medication and it was clear to me that her medication was not to be mixed with any alcohol whatsoever. Barbara seemed to be very relaxed and casually asked me about my past life. She wanted to know more about the book which I was writing. Maybe my first marriage as well as the second, would have survived had I told my wives what really happened to me more than 10 years prior to meeting and marrying them.

Maybe I didn't want to be pitied for all the dramas I went through. Back in 1996 there were still floppy discs in use which I mastered quite well. Barbara was an expert in that field and had already rapidly progressed onto Microsoft Windows operating system. She asked me about my password for my PC and I knew instantly that she was probably trying to go into my PC files without my permission whilst she was in my flat alone. I switched the PC on and tried to access my files but the 'manager' of my software blocked the access because there were too many attempts made with an incorrect password. I could feel my blood pressure rising and had to go out of the flat and took Duke for a walk. It took me some 10 minutes to calm down and try to think clearly about the situation. I came to the conclusion that Barbara was already very ill and she had just done something that probably any woman in the same predicament would do. I convinced myself that it was just her nosiness and inquisitiveness and not necessarily anything nasty.

When I asked, why she wanted to look at my private files she just said that she wanted to read some of my written pages to see what the book was about. My e-mail account was also blocked at the same time. I thanked God that at least the other details of my bank account and the rest of the other private documents were safe. I asked myself if there was any point in talking to Barbara at all till the morning. My gut instinct was telling me no and my heart was telling me yes. I chose to listen to my heart and hear her explanation in its entirety.

She apologised and apologised again and again and burst into tears. I thought that maybe my approach was too hard and maybe Barbara was simply, as mentioned, just inquisitive and wanted to see why I didn't tell her about my past life. I felt that I was in command of my emotions and said that she would never see the book until it was published. She went all quiet and wanted to go to bed. All she said before going to the bathroom was how stupid it had been of her, ruining the chance to get closer to me. I didn't say a word and went to make myself comfortable on the sofa and dozed off.

At about 2am I could hear her phone ringing in my bedroom and heard her saying that she would be out in a moment. Be out in a moment? My mind was racing and I realised that she had rung BBC transport to have a driver outside my flat to pick her up! I quickly put my trousers on and grabbed my jacket and went to the bedroom. Barbara was fully dressed and had all the rest of her belongings in her big shopping bag. She went past me and headed for the front door and off she went! Not a word, no explanation, nothing!

In a sense I was glad but at the same time became worried about what she was going to do next. Would she cancel all the journeys booked with my company? Would she say malicious things about me to her co-workers? I thought 'to hell with it!' I began talking to myself and my pet Duke just looked at me. On many occasions I scolded him but only when he did something silly that could harm him, as for example trying to cross the road ahead of me. I carried on talking loudly and my voice sounded frustrated. He just lay there and there was a fear in his eyes. He had just experienced a different me and couldn't figure out whether my loud talking was directed at him or not. I slowly calmed down and called my office to say all my work for that day should be cancelled. Luckily, there weren't any important jobs lined up for me. I decided to have a good drink of Scotch and stay in bed for as long as possible. I switched off all the mobiles and the land line in case someone wanted to contact me and disturb my sleep. This happened on a few occasions when I was faced with the dilemma of what to do next.

Duke came to my side with his tail wagging which told me that he wasn't frightened any more. I poured myself a second glass of whiskey and tried to concentrate on the sequence of events that led to Barbara leaving me in the middle of the night. I could find no reason to blame myself and came to the conclusion that it was Barbara's fault, because she tried to access my computer files behind my back. There were never any pornographic images, nor any other 'grey area' videos stored on that or any other PC for that matter and it had nothing to do with morality. I just didn't have the time or need to watch all the 'fake orgasms.' The strong neat drink was slowly affecting my clear thinking and I was drifting into a deep sleep.

I must have slept for some 7-8 hours when Duke woke me up, licking my face which meant that he had to be taken out for his morning 'walkies.' Once outside of my place I hailed a taxi and took Duke to Hyde Park. I just didn't want to drive knowing that the alcohol I had drunk some 8 hours before would impair my judgement in all that London traffic. Duke was running back and forth, happy to be with me. After all he had been my pet for over 11 years, and I was his 'leader of the pack.'

The whole time, whilst walking in the park I tried to make sense of what had happened some 9 hours before with Barbara. To be quite frank I at that moment couldn't give a damn. She was the one who broke the fragile bond between me and her by trying to invade my privacy on my PC. She in my mind was deleted! No more answering her calls, no more driving her home, no more contacts with her whatsoever. A few months passed and apart from her few phone calls, my life stabilised a bit, but I was still working intensively on my move to the USA. This was all that was on my mind.

A lot of my decisions in the past were made on the spur of the moment. Some were good and some were absolutely ridiculous, precarious and potentially deadly. Anyhow after a few days of careful thinking about all the possible pros and cons I decided definitely to go back to USA and become a flight instructor. I liked the idea and wanted it to happen as soon as possible.

Of course, I would have to refresh my flying and piloting abilities and pass all the additional exams. The idea looked to me to be very attractive and exciting! Not because of what happened between Barbara and myself on that night. We weren't intimate at all and I didn't even have any urge to have a sexual relationship with her. I just couldn't imagine myself being Barbara's carer. There were no selfish reasons nor any lack of compassion towards Barbara. There simply was nothing that would tie me to her. I felt, in some ways, sorry for her but that was all. There was no love, instead, only a suspicion about her in general. There was also an element of one of my mid-life crisis.

I had no family of my own and had nothing to lose by going away for a few months or years. The BBC would always renew my contract, since they knew that my working records were impeccable. I began to set my plans in motion. My only worry was my pet Duke and what to do with the shop in Brick Lane. I had a nephew back in Slovenia who was out of work and maybe he could look after the shop and care for Duke in the meanwhile? I decided not to tell Barbara about my plans. I was thinking I would rent out my flat in West London and my nephew Sasha could live above the shop in Brick Lane.

I arranged to have a discussion about my plan with the second cab company, with which I also had a contract. They also promised that their doors would always be open for me. I began to contact some letting agencies around my area and they had lots of professional people on their files who were looking for accommodation near their place of work. I contacted my old flight academy in Florida whom I passed my flight test with and they were delighted to have me as their prospective employee as an instructor. I scaled down my driving for the BBC whilst organising my necessary paper work regarding the US visa requirements.

There was some £25000 in my bank account which according to my calculation was enough to cover the cost of a return flight to US and the necessary instructor's flight training. In my second account was also a substantial amount of money left to cover all my direct debits for various insurances, electricity, gas, shop rent in short for almost all expenditure whilst I would be away. In the event of letting my flat through the agency that money would cover any emergency expenditure. I just wanted to make sure that all the financial commitments were met. In the following 3 weeks, there were no calls from Barbara which surprised me. I didn't wish anything bad to happen to her. After all she was not my enemy.

My dispatchers were ringing me every second day and enquiring when I would be available to take on some work but no mention of requests from Barbara for driving her to and from her home in St Albans. None of her work colleagues had cancelled any of their journeys which pleased me. I was hoping that the whole 'episode with Barbara was over once and for all. The US visa was issued without any problems and the next thing to be done was to inform my nephew in Slovenia that he should prepare himself to come to the UK.

3

The Journeys With Jill Dando

Within days one of the letting agencies had already lined up 3 prospective tenants to come and view the flat. My work was scaled down to a minimum. A few days went by and I received a phone call from the cab company 'Niven Cars' and they asked me to come to their offices in Lime Grove, Shepherds Bush, W12. It was about a prospective driver who had been recommended by me a week earlier. The manager took me to his office and enquired about that prospective driver. I told him how we met on a few occasions at the BBC and how he approached and asked me if he could join 'Niven Cars' hire company, because he wasn't happy with the company he worked for at present. He was smartly dressed and had a nice S class Mercedes. I went further to say that he appeared to be a very friendly person. He supposedly came from Serbia, at least his accent sounded Serbian and had some relatives in Slovenia and I added, "that's all I know about him." At the end of my conversation with the manager, I jokingly added: "By the way he is not my 'boyfriend' and the company should make further enquiries about this driver."

There were some customers who wanted me to drive them privately and some even offered to make me their permanent driver, something akin to a butler but I turned it down, because I didn't want to end up being a servant. I enjoyed offering and selling my service (not sexual service). Some of my passengers explained the reason why they had asked if I did any private work, namely because some cab companies were reckless with some of their customers detail's. Their addresses were sometimes passed on to other drivers and inevitably passengers' details would be compromised and sometimes passed on to the paparazzi.

For those reasons, Jill Dando, after driving her a few times previously, asked if I did any private work. She didn't fully understand the law that governs the cab and taxi trade. It took a few minutes for her to understand my limitations as a PCO driver. There was also a point of morality since I had met her through Niven Cars, and it would look bad on me doing private jobs behind the company's back which also treated me honourably. She was also travelling with our BBC Company. Jill took it on board that in the event of an accident my insurance would be rendered as void because the booking wasn't logged with a company which had an operators' licence. Jill wasn't looking for a cheap ride but just didn't like some of the receptionists and drivers at Niven cars.

She also suspected that sometimes there were photographers outside venues such as 'The Ivy' restaurant when the only people who knew where she was travelling to, were Niven's receptionists! Because of that she often had to go to the next street and hail a black cab to take her around the block and walk the last few yards to where she wanted to go without any intrusion. Of course, according to her, there were sometimes problems with people wanting her autograph while hailing a black taxi. I asked her why it was she trusted me since I worked for the same company. She just said that she heard from people like Clive James, Tony Benn and others, that I am a trustworthy person and do not talk about my passengers. Jill admitted that she had in the past tested me by asking me about other passengers and was impressed, how skilfully

I avoided talking about any of my past passengers. She was telling the truth, since I never spoke about my passengers to anybody, not even Barbara. I told Jill to give me time to work something out that would be within the law. The plan took some thinking and a lot of combinations just to make sure that it was all 'above board' and legal.

On my next journey with Jill I revealed the plan and she was very happy to go along with it. She would simply ring me and I would call my booking office with a different destination. I didn't mind taking her some extra miles further without adding extra charges. There was also a danger that booking receptionists would suspect that something was going on between Jill and myself. There was absolutely nothing, apart from the reasons just explained, going on between us. There was only one problem, namely that I couldn't always at any given moment drop what I was doing and be where Jill wanted me to be.

For some unknown reason, she always sat in the front seat, but every so often I noticed, as an ex driving instructor, that her right foot went down on her 'imaginary' gas pedal. It happened if someone was fast approaching our car, although my car had tinted windows and it was hard to see who was inside. Only a driving instructor is able to make those observations, because he or she must have good peripheral vision of at least 60 degrees in order to act on pupil's possible wrong body movements especially when behind the steering wheel. A pupils' right leg movement obviously indicates which pedal will be used and can be lethal, also deadly if the gas pedal is pressed instead of the brake pedal. Jill's right foot on the 'gas' pedal obviously indicated that she wanted to move faster.

My observation obviously had nothing to do with admiring 'someone's legs' and I am not in the slightest promoting any 'conspiracy.' I have never dared to ask her, if she was frightened of something or somebody and come to think of it, perhaps I should have. In as much as I liked Jill's custom, the short journeys simply weren't warranting enough income. I was toying with the idea that the Serbian driver whom I introduced some weeks before to Niven cars, would be ideal to drive her on those occasions in case of my move to the USA. The problem was that I didn't want to take the risk since the driver Vojo wasn't known to me long enough to trust him. Anyhow, I arranged a meeting with Vojo and had a lengthy conversation. We spoke about Ex-Yugoslavia and what made him come to the UK. I was a bit puzzled by his opinion about the UK in general. He didn't particularly like this country and blamed the Western governments for the breakup of Yugoslavia. Apparently, he was living in Acton in a rented room in a house owned by another Serb whom I also met many years before at the Serbian Orthodox church in Ladbroke Grove West London. I came to the conclusion that, with his attitude towards the UK and The West, he wouldn't succeed.

Deep down I began to have doubts whether he was the right man to be with Niven Cars at all. Niven, the proprietor of Niven Cars, had most of his work coming from the BBC. My 'hope was that the moment Vojo made the slightest mistake it would be my recommendation to get rid of him immediately. From then on I just disliked Vojo. He knew that I drove Barbara to St Albans quite often and even had the cheek to ask me whether she was my partner. I told him not to ask me such a question. On my next visit to the BBC he came over to me in the foyer and wanted to know how to get similar jobs, like driving Dr Owen, Jill Dando, Bob Stewart and others that I had on my books. He knew that I drove many more high profile people. I must admit that on that occasion I lost my temper and told him to p**s off and that he should not approach me again unless asked! That put an end to my connection with him and I didn't see him for a while. I slowed down even more with my work, as I was busy with organising my trip to the USA.

The next problem came along with Barbara's demand to see me urgently. I was worried that she had some bad news about her illness. She booked her journey back to St Albans and when she got into the car, immediately started to question me about my plans of going to The States. Knowing her condition, I didn't mind waiting, until she finished with her emotional outburst. The moment she paused I got a chance to raise my voice and asked her to stop talking and asked what my private life had to do with her? "You disappeared for nearly 3 weeks and are now insisting that I ask permission to go to USA." With tears running down her cheeks she said that she had plans to be my partner. I was supposedly a very reliable, honest and hard-working person and she would make me happy. "I am still young enough to have a child with you" were Barbara's soft spoken words as she wiped away her tears. Suddenly some strange thoughts entered my mind. I wanted to forget all about the bad feelings I had about her. I told myself that maybe Barbara and I could work something out between us. Maybe all my distrust was meaningless or baseless. Or perhaps I was being too sensitive?

I started my car and we drove off towards her home. After a while

Barbara asked if there was something she said, that had upset me. "I just need some time to think about all this," was my reply. At least she stopped crying and before long we reached her home safely. As she was leaving the car she quickly planted a kiss on my cheek. I didn't know what to say and briskly said good night and drove off.

During the whole drive back to my London pad, Barbara's words were still ringing in my ears. I kept talking to myself about how ridiculous it would be to live with Barbara. How would my world change and what would happen to my wish to meet a lady that had the same interests as me? What would happen to my interest in classical music with a partner that finds going to a classical theatre performance boring? I realised that it would also be impossible for me to handle her medical needs. It sounds as if I was selfish but to be with a person with MS there must be a strong bond and love on both sides. It's one thing that Barbara was earning in excess of £45k a year and was paying her mortgage and financed her son's study but what would happen when her medical condition progressed. I also had to consider that in the event things wouldn't work out and in the case of me walking away, leaving her, she would be vulnerable. I decided to give us time and I meant, a lot of time.

The next evening, Duke was excited to see me as usual. We had a good dinner and afterwards he just wouldn't leave my side. He kept looking at me and I knew he wanted to tell me something. To distract him I went to play a piece on the piano. In the middle of the piece I was playing, he jumped on the keyboard. He had never done it before and although it really didn't bother me, it convinced me that he desperately wanted to tell me something. The only thing I remembered was that for a short while he kept running around my bed and wanted to crawl underneath it, but there was not enough space. I checked it a few times but could see nothing.

When I was a boy, I had lots of homing pigeons and one in particular by the name of Bixie. That pigeon woke me up one morning whilst fighting with another pigeon on the window ledge. With any animal as a pet there is a kind of understanding and relationship developed between the owner and the pet. Bixie was my pet which I reared from just 2 weeks old. Still to this day, I am convinced that my pigeon pet saved my life, when my father argued with and slapped my mother in the face. He was convicted of altering a lottery-raffle ticket in order to try to win a star prize which was a motorbike. He kept his conviction secret and not all letters were delivered to our house. A few months afterwards, my mother told me that she intercepted one of the court's letters and confronted him with it on that morning. Because my pigeon Bixie woke me up I could hear how my father's army pistol was cocked. The pistol with which I had played many times. I knew the sound of a loud click! Whilst my father shouted in my parent's room 'where is Olga?' my younger sister, I sensed that something terrible was about to happen. I jumped on my first floor window ledge where Bixie, my pigeon, was still flapping his wings and jumped on the closest branch of our huge cherry tree next to the window. Only years later, my aunty and my mother confirmed that had my sister Olga been at home at the time, my father would have shot my mother first, then my brother Thomas, then Olga, me and then himself! Obviously and subsequently I was never the same again and the frightening episode changed my life for ever!

4

Barbara & Her Drugs

I had an eerie feeling and was convinced that Duke was warning me of something and was determined to find out what bothered him. After so many years since my pet pigeon warned me of imminent danger, I could sense my pet Duke was definitely trying to tell me the same. I went all over my flat and checked all the electrical appliances. I checked my gas heater and the cooker, but Duke kept running towards the bed. Still puzzled, I had another closer look in my bedroom and another under my bed. Right in the far corner there was a small carrier bag. I used a broom stick and got it out. It reeked of drugs. Duke started to bark and wanted to tear into the already half ripped open carrier bag. He must have tried to drag it from underneath the bed many times before and at least the reason for Duke's barking was explained. But why didn't I smell the drug before and why didn't I take any notice, since Duke did try to crawl under the bed quite a few times?. Duke must have reached the well wrapped plastic carrier bag very recently and maybe I was too tired to smell anything. I must confess that on this occasion I failed to smell it sooner.

During all the years with the BBC and other companies I watched some of the passengers, not necessarily all BBC employees, finishing their joints before entering my car. Now I suddenly faced a problem. I had to find out if Barbara had left the substantial amount of cannabis on purpose or if she had just forgotten and left it behind. The second problem was to find out whether she was a dealer and if so, how deep she was involved. Suddenly in the eyes of the law I was in possession of class A B C drug or any other class for that matter and it was in my property!

"Holy cow," I uttered loudly and asked myself what do I do? After

it all sunk in my first reaction was to be angry and upset. Then came the fear. Fear of possibly being arrested for possession of some type of drug which wasn't even mine!

Still really furious I decided to call Barbara immediately and ask her what the hell she was thinking bringing drugs to my place. Barbara answered my call straight away and didn't seem to be worried about what I found at all. I told her to call me back when she was alone and able to talk. She called me back after a short while and I told her that I wanted to meet her after she finished her work.

At 9pm I was in my car outside the BBC Wood Lane W12 and she got into the car. She just barked "What was that all about?" I then became enraged and hissed back at her "You have a cheek to ask that when there is a small carrier bag with some pungent smelling dope sitting in my home that belongs to you!" I drove around the corner into a leafy side road, where I was able to safely park. If she hadn't stopped telling me about my paranoia, I would have driven her back to the BBC and left her there. I had to hold my hands in my pockets due to the uncontrollable trembling. I was surprised that I was considering slapping her in the face. I calmed down and changed tactics by telling her how I had served twice on a jury before I met her. I wanted to let her know that I knew quite a lot about court cases and the results of people being found guilty of drug possession and other felonies.

I just wanted to know whether she was aware of the consequences of being in possession of a classified drug or drugs. She just seemed to be oblivious of the gravity of what she was doing. My next question was, who she was buying the drugs from. Apparently, her son was taking care of that side.

I suddenly felt like I was sitting with a person who had a very serious

illness, leaving some kind of drug on my premises and had a son who was probably hooked on drugs himself! I was livid with the thought of being caught with a person who was in possession of drugs. Luckily my self- preservation instinct cut in immediately and in my mind the plan was worked out in a split second. Barbara was seemingly always dropping things, which I had put it down to her medication and didn't spot her dependency. She burst into tears and asked me to take her home. My plan was different and therefore I insisted that her small plastic carrier bag had to be collected first from my place.

Whilst we drove to my place, I suggested that while she was waiting outside my pad to collect her carrier bag, she should ring the BBC transport and book her journey with me to St Albans. It took a minute to ask my neighbours to look after Duke and then I picked up the small bag where the drug or drugs were and wiped it clean with a damp cloth so that there were no finger prints. While doing this I loudly cursed the moment I met Barbara! I felt like a criminal cleaning that little bag of my own fingerprints as if it was mine! The main thing was to get rid of that damn bag! I sensed a feeling of relief but there was still the whole journey to her home ahead of us. I checked my brake lights, which I had never done before. I wanted to be sure that there was nothing wrong with the front and side lights as well in case the police stopped us on the motorway. Any policeman would be able to smell the cannabis. By now the smell was spreading throughout the car. She didn't say a word for a good while and that suited me just fine.

As we stopped outside her house she said sorry again and was beginning to explain why and how difficult it was for her go through with her MS on a daily basis. "Zinco, please don't be upset and I know

that it was a mistake to leave the little bag behind. I am not a drug dealer and my son is only trying to help me so that I don't have to go to drug pushers." Out of the blue, I was inadvertently involved with a BBC employee, her son using drugs and just the thought of how my life could have changed with one simple random check-stop by the police, sent shivers down my spine! As Duke and I entered the flat, he immediately went to the bedroom and sniffed around the area where a while ago that little plastic bag was. I jokingly spoke to him and said that he would be an asset to the police as a sniffer dog. I gave him a large portion of steamed fillet of cod and the same for me. The last thing I needed was a call from Barbara and thus switched off my two phones.

There was a third phone which was only for an emergency and of which Barbara hadn't been given the number. I felt exhausted but nevertheless wanted to calm down by playing something on my piano. Duke didn't jump on the piano keys on this occasion which pleased me. He was by now behaving differently. I found an excuse and as usual when I faced any big problem, I poured myself an extra-large gin and tonic. I found it easier to think of my next move and search for a solution. It was well past 2 am and I finally fell asleep. Duke usually would wake me up at 6 or 7am but the next morning it was as if he sensed that I needed some more sleep and woke me up at 9am instead.

As we walked to Hyde Park, the events of the night before were slowly playing in my mind and I wanted to make some sense of it all. The big questions kept cropping up of what to do? What could be done? What will I do? I decided to drive to the Niven Cars company and see if any jobs were lined up for me. Sir David Frost made a request for

me to drive him to the Houses of Parliament that afternoon and wait for him at the Houses of Parliament and take him back to his home in Kensington. He arranged that I could have a coffee in the guests' area. It was my third time having a coffee there. This job was easy and obviously well paid. However, I couldn't just wander around the Palace of Westminster as freely as if I was at the BBC TV Centre.

For the security sensitive jobs like being a driver to Mr Tony Benn, Betty Boothroyd, Mr Livingstone, to name a few, I am sure that both, the BBC and Niven Cars had done some kind of background checks on me. I felt privileged to be close to some very well-known and important people. I presumed that the company with which I had a short contract in Docklands did the same checks, since I drove a lot of MI5 personnel. No, I didn't end up agent 007 for those reasons. I was ready to slap Barbara around the face after discovering the cannabis back in my place. Had I tolerated something illegal like that in Barbara's case, my contract, privileges and my handsome income would have been lost instantly.

All my life I have taken care of not to get involved in any crime. Yes, in my turbulent youth in order to survive back in my country of birth, Slovenia, I did some cinema ticket-touting which was only an offence, not a crime. Did I in my childhood help myself to some of the neighbour's strawberries or peaches? Yes, I did. There was always somebody coming to my shop in Brick Lane offering me some stuff for sale. There were expensive works of art going for a silly sum. A sure sign that the items were stolen. Nobody sells expensive old paintings on Sunday Street market at 5am! Although I am not a connoisseur in the subject of old paintings, nevertheless I have seen lots and lots of these, enough to give an estimated value. Had I bought any of the

'non-kosher' artefacts, it wouldn't be a case of pinching some of the neighbour's strawberries.

To say it again, this book is not about my honesty and I am not remarking on what a good person I am. I have my faults like any other person, and without any criminal record.

Barbara didn't ring me on that day and she hadn't rung for a further few days and I was thinking that finally she had found somebody else and that pleased me. She also didn't ring me over the following two weeks. Even receptionists at my booking office were asking me why Barbara had stopped driving with me. There wasn't any complaint made about me in relation to Barbara and I simply commented that she was probably on holiday. Certainly, I wasn't telling them about the incident with the drugs left at my place. As usual my lips were sealed. It's obvious that in the period of over 12 years I had heard and seen things that could raise eyebrows. Sometimes there were passengers, not necessarily connected to the BBC, making love on the back seat and I had to ask the passengers to reimburse me for having to pay for the 'deep clean' because of 'the white love honey' they left behind! But who am I to divulge the names of those people who had trusted me with their lives literally! I could go on, who and to which private clubs in Mayfair were my passengers going, but would these revelations serve any purpose? I have also not included any gossip, hence all the events written about had really and truly happened.

And there was the notorious British paedophile, a necrophiliac, Jimmy Saville who over a period of years had sexually abused countless young boys and two young girls. Most personnel at the BBC knew this, including Barbara, but I can clearly state that had Jimmy Saville, whilst I drove him to Stoke Mandeville Hospital on more

than one occasion, asked or hinted in any way if I were interested in any of his activities, I would absolutely have revealed it by now, without a shadow of doubt!

Yes, I didn't like him from the moment I met him, knowing the rumours about his activities, but my book is not based on rumours, it's based on facts. I wasn't surprised when he also asked me if I did any private work. To drive somebody privately in the UK is almost impossible, because anybody driving 'for hire and reward' needs a hire and reward insurance policy, 'operators' licence, which requires a base office and a host of other requirements. Were there rumours that some of the BBC researchers knew about his despicable acts? Yes. But why haven't those BBC employees gone to report to their superiors? Were there rumours about some Christmas parties, where some drunk males and females, ITN, ITV, GEC, BBC employees were riding on the tops of giant Xerox photocopying machines and had their genitals photocopied? Yes, but these were only rumours and gossip and I wasn't privy to those incidents, despite seeing some of the 'Xerox' copies. Whilst on the subject about rumours, on many occasions I had driven the very same people, rumours about whom were going around. I didn't dare tell them and I am glad because God knows how I couldn't close 'Pandora's Box' and how those individuals would have reacted.

There were occasions, when I was able to tell if a male or female executive passenger was going to be unfaithful behind their partner's or husband's backs. Usually, they would change the destination and before long, we would end up in front of a hotel of some sort. On those occasions I had to be extra careful and fold my daily sheet in such a way that only a signature box was visible, just in case their 'other half'

would drive with me on the same day. I wanted at all costs to protect my reputation as 'Zinco, the man with sealed lips.'

It was one of those busy days, but I felt great, because an hour ago, after I brought Anthea Turner to HRH Prince Charles's Highgrove Estate and whilst drinking a cup of tea, the Prince came to say hello to three of us drivers. There was just enough time to tell him, how I met his brother Prince Andrew at his Windsor residence and quickly added that one day I'll write a book, and I could see his bemusement. We were served an array of sandwiches, snacks and hot drinks, just the same as I experienced with Prince Andrew's hospitality.

My phone rang and I answered it without looking at the number shown. It was my sister in law from Slovenia asking me to come to Slovenia as soon as possible due to my brother's stage 4 of pancreatic cancer and that my brother Thomas wanted to see me. She couldn't tell me how much time he had left but hoped a few weeks. It really shook me. And if that wasn't enough bad news, she went on to say how my father was also diagnosed with bowel cancer. I told her that I would be there as soon as I possibly could. But she had additional bad news. My favourite aunty was also critically ill due to her diabetes and thrombosis in her leg. Father at that time, was 86 years old and had no history of any kind of illness throughout his life. As far as I knew there was no history of any cancer illnesses in our family and now suddenly out of the blue, I was dealt a triple 'whammy' of three family members suffering from cancer and infection at almost the same time!

My concentration on staying in the lane was failing me and I had to stop at the very same service station where I had a puncture a good while ago whilst driving Barbara home for the first time. After having a short rest and a strong espresso I pressed on towards home. It was

almost 2am when, after collecting Duke, I briefly went through my post and poured myself a triple gin and tonic and began to slowly take in all that had happened in the past few hours. In an instant my outlook on life was changed. Illness, sorrow and the prospect of inevitable funerals were looming in my mind. I booked an online return flight to Slovenia on the earliest available flight which would leave in less than two days. After another drink I fell asleep but only to be awaken by Duke.

I decided to take him to my neighbours although he kept looking at me as if to say 'why?' He must have sensed that something wasn't right and probably sensed my sombre mood. I had to concentrate on what was needed to be done before my trip. The 'to do' list was quite long. My flight academy in Florida, the BBC operations manager, Niven cars, the credit card companies and a myriad of other companies had to be contacted. It took hours on the phone before most of the items from my long list were ticked off.

I then rang Barbara and spoke slowly about my brother Thomas's cancer and about my father's cancer as well and made her aware of my forthcoming travel to Slovenia. All she said was that it was normal for people above a certain age to end up with cancer. There was not a word of any sympathy or empathy. Nothing whatsoever. I was taken aback by her lack of empathy but I was pleased with myself that I was able to understand her present state of mind. She was to be discharged the very next day, but she had virtually no close friends and I began to pity her. She then quietly began to cry. There was nothing I could do and said that she would be all right until my return and rang off. Whilst driving with Duke towards Hyde Park I noticed dizziness and a sense of morbidity.

5

Death Of My Beloved Brother & Duke

Duke was running to and fro and seemed to be happy with me in the park. My phone was ringing every 5 minutes. The calls came from Slovenia, estate agents, a car hire company, BBC external operations, Westminster City Council and others. After my last call was finished, I looked to see where Duke was. He would often wander off but not too far. I spotted him across the road in Hyde Park-Serpentine and he was waiting for the traffic lights to change at the pedestrian crossing. At that very moment I was glad that I taught him how to wait at the pedestrian crossing and only cross when people started to cross. He would then walk along with them to the other side of the road safely. At that moment there was nobody waiting but he knew how to wait and listen to the bleeping sound and only then would he cross. I had heard the bleep upon which Duke began to cross the road. Out of nowhere came a SUV with a woman driver and Duke's last look at me was if to ask me what to do. I screamed 'NO! No! No!' But all I could see was his tail still wagging from under one of the wheels. I ran across the road and was nearly hit by a car myself.

The woman driver had obviously jumped the red light and when she saw Duke crossing, tried to stop, but it was too late for Duke. She immediately admitted that it was her fault. I burst into tears as did she, wanting to console me. I refused. Still crying, I just barked at her to move her 'f....g car so that I could pick up Duke's dead, lifeless body from underneath the rear wheel. With my eyes shut and soaked in tears, I heard my Duke's bones crushing as the woman moved her SUV forward. I took a blanket out of my car and covered Duke's dead body, right in the middle of the road.

Two drivers stepped out of their cars and began to talk to the woman driver and I could clearly see that they were visibly upset by what they saw. They also scolded the woman for jumping the red light. They asked me if there was anything they could do and I thanked them and told them that there was nothing to help me with. A passing police car stopped on the opposite side of the road to see why the traffic had stopped. When two officers saw my Duke's little tail protruding from underneath the blanket one of the officers went to direct the traffic whilst I picked up Duke's body and placed him on the grass verge. Another officer spoke to the woman driver and then to the two drivers who were driving behind her and he took their short statement. The road was slowly getting clear again and I could see that the woman driver was genuinely upset and was willing to take a breath test and it was clear. She was beginning to shake and sat down on the same grass verge not far from where Duke was lying still covered with the blanket. The two drivers who were driving behind her had agreed and confirmed to the police that the woman driver indeed jumped the red light.

The two officers were marvellous and told me my rights and that I could ask for the woman driver to be charged for her reckless driving and the loss of Duke. I said that pressing the charges wouldn't bring my Duke back any way. I am glad that I didn't press the charges since she was equally visibly shocked by what she had done. One of the officers called his base in Hyde Park and told me that they would take care of Duke's body. I touched my Duke for the last time and left for home.

My neighbours were, which was unusual, standing outside their flat and saw tears in my eyes and asked me where Duke was and I told them that Duke will never come to see them again. They also burst into tears. They knew him well and had cared for Duke many times, for almost 3 years and were also crying. I had a sudden urge to go back to my flat and be left alone. Unfortunately for the woman driver, 'in my mind', she had punished herself enough and I am sure that the guilt will be with her for the rest of her life. To this day I still maintain that women are in general better drivers than men. Period. My Duke is buried somewhere in Hyde Park according to the Parks police because it happened in one of the Crown parks. All I had left was my Duke's collar and photos.

I wasn't actually in a state to do anything except grab the first tall glass available and fill it with red wine. Of course, I was getting worried that my heavy drinking on three occasions in the past two weeks could lead me to become an alcoholic. I swore to myself that I would drink less in the future. I have always waited for at least ten hours before doing any driving after I had a drink.

When I woke up the next morning still in the haze of what happened on the previous day, the whole episode came back, when I realised, there was no Duke next to my bed. It was only then that I realised that everything that happened in the last thirty six hours was a brutal truth. My father was dying from cancer, so was my brother Thomas and Auntie Hanna and my Duke gone!

My first thought was to sell the flat since there were too many memories to remind me of Duke. The following morning I rang the estate agents' office and told them to stop interviewing and rather begin looking for a buyer. My reasons appeared to the agent to be plausible and I assured him that there would be no change of mind. He was prepared to wait until my return from abroad. He told me that my flat would sell immediately since he had a lot of buyers waiting on his books. I was surprised by how my mood changed so suddenly and the sale of my flat would lessen the pain and alleviate the loss of my Duke.

The decision about the sale was made and there was no going back. For the rest of my day I was busy packing my suitcase, making sure that on the day of my departure all the electrics except the fridge would be switched off. The list was endless. I opened the fridge and the first prepared meal was Duke's! I quickly grabbed all his meals and his basket and went downstairs to the main road and binned all of his food and his basket.

For the remaining few hours I just walked and wandered around my area, sad and did not really know what to do next until my journey to the airport. My flight to Slovenia was delayed. Eventually I was on the way to my home town some 90 miles from the airport. It was almost midnight when my sister-in-law met me at the hotel. My brother, because of his deteriorating condition wasn't restricted to any visiting hours. When he saw me the expressions on his face told me that he was really pleased to see me. It was nearly two years since we had seen each other. From seeing all the tubes inserted in both of his hands and in other parts of his body I knew that he wouldn't last long. He was a different brother from how I remembered him before. He asked me to sit beside him and wanted to know how I was doing. He asked me about my work at the BBC and how proud he was to have a brother who was 'mingling' with some of the world renowned and important people.

On the advice of my sister-in-law, I wasn't to tell him about our father's condition. Despite all the medication including morphine he was quite alert. He went on to say how he was looking forward to very soon being out of the hospital and how he'd pick the grapes in his small vineyard and make wine again. They had a beautiful house just outside our town in a very quiet area surrounded by woodland. I remember eating the 'Porcini' mushroom goulash, mushrooms foraged in those nearby woods. He then suddenly went quiet, maybe because of the strong dose of morphine. My sister in law looked at me in a horror and pointed at my brother's eyes. His lovely eyes were not blinking at all and they stared at the ceiling. My sister-in-law grabbed me by my arm and began to pray. I pressed the emergency button and 3-4 nurses rushed to his bed. My sister in law became hysterical and I didn't know what to do. Because we two were never really close I didn't want to drive her back home. Obviously by then I was in tears as well. She asked to call her best two female friends. It was logical to me they would be best suited for the occasion.

The funeral took place two days afterwards. He was very popular in our town and many people attended. The day after was a day to visit my father. We weren't speaking for decades due to the near tragedy all those decades ago, when he threatened our whole family with his gun. He wasn't in bad shape at all despite having cancer. Being his son, I was able to find out his diagnosis and hear the prognosis. The personnel at the retirement home were very helpful. They confirmed in front of him, how he often spoke about his lost son (meaning me), and whenever there was a concert arranged for the occupants, how his son Zdenko used to

Just a few of my past clients...

Sir Kenneth Charles Branagh
Actor, Director, Film Producer and
Screenwriter

With thanks
for all your
help & kindness
– see you soon,

John Simpson
Correspondent

Lord Robert Runcie
Former Archbishop of Canterbury

Zenko
with my thanks indeed

Robert Hardy
98

Robert Hardy CBE FSA
British Actor

Mr Boris
Johnson

xx

Boris Johnson
British Prime Minister

Julian Lloyd Webber
British Solo Cellist

Russ Abbot
British Musician, Comedian and Actor

Dame Patricia Routledge, DBE
British Actress, Comedian and Singer

Ruby Wax, OBE
American Actress, Comedian, Mental Health Campaigner, Lecturer and Author

Angela May Rippon, CBE
British Television Journalist, Newsreader, Writer and Presenter.

Jilly Cooper, CBE
English Author

Julia Mary Fownes Somerville, Lady Dixon, OBE
British Television News Reader and Reporter

Me and my master Duke

The pre-flight check before the solo flight to Orlando

```
-------------------------------- Job  36146 ------------------------------
Acc    808 JILL DANDO                    Normal        Service C  CAR
Contact                      Ref                   Tel

TERMINAL 4 LHR
NOTE:JILL DANDO
[
[
  Controller [W4 - LHR                    ]         ---------- CLIENT - DRIV
  Job Type PreBook  Booked for 10/04/1998 Fri 12:40   Pricing -------- -----
             Appearance Time 10/04/1998 Fri 00:09   Distance  ------    ----
     Job Taken by MICHAEL  on 09/04/1998 Thu 17:11     Price  -------    ----
     Allocated by -------- on                 --:--   W/Time   0 -------  ----
Amended by --------  Started              --:--      Extras  -------   ----
                      Completed             --:--    Totals: -------   ----
   Driver  ZA1                         No.          VAT Band 01 17.5%
CIRCUIT Pickup 0  Drop 0  Delay   0 Add Delays  0  -----------------------
   PODs required No          Deleted No  COAed No
   Cleared to Pay No      Paid            Pay No.
   Cleared to Inv No  Invoiced          Inv. No.
-------------------------------------------------------------------------
```

One of Jill Dando's journeys with me on 10th April 1998

Dear Zinco,

Thank you for your recent e-mail - Henriette Guthauser returned to her native Switzerland some time ago and I have replaced her as Clive's PA.

I passed your message on to Clive, who regrets that he is too sick to respond in person. He remembers you well and asked me to send you his thanks for thinking of him and very best wishes for the future.

Kind regards,

Susie Young

Just one of the emails recieved from Clive James AO CBE FRSL critic, journalist, broadcaster and writer

For Zdenko,
All Best Wishes
from the Jungle Queen
Carol Thatcher
Dec 2005

Carol Thatcher is an English journalist, author and media personality of note play a piece of music just as good as that group on his accordion and piano. I was amused to hear all this, but the damage was done all those years ago when he also accused my mother of adultery and claiming I was an illegitimate child. I looked at our relationship as him being someone related to me rather than my father.

At the end of our conversation in private I just said that my 'war with him was over' and promised to be back the next day. The next sad moment was when my favourite Auntie Hanna at the hospital, but hadn't recognised me and all I could do was to kiss her forehead and leave.

I rang my sister, whom I met in town and had a very lengthy conversation with her. She just couldn't get over the fact that the Yugoslav communist system was over, of which she was a member and had a lot of privileges, such as almost free holidays by the Adriatic Sea. She simply forgot that after good times always come bad times. She really sounded very negative and showed no emotion whilst I tried to tell her some of my tragedies. At least I tried to make her understand that my life wasn't always a bed of roses. She even commented that the loss of my beloved Duke was only 'losing a dog!' I nearly bit my tongue and realised that we were worlds apart. By the way, at that time lots of people in Slovenia still kept their dogs on a chain. Even as a child I often got into trouble by freeing my grandmother's dog from his chain and felt sad when he got chained again. The law was later changed and I am glad to say how now in Slovenia it is a criminal offence to chain up any dog.

It became obvious that Olga was bent on annoying me and it was time for me to go. I found an excuse and shook her hand and left.

She subsequently tried to reach me over the phone but I decided not to answer her call. I just wanted us to leave things where we left them and couldn't wait to return to my hotel and try to get my flight changed to an earlier date. I managed to rebook it for the day after next. There were many people calling me and inviting me to their homes. Family members, neighbours, school friends and friends as well and there was simply no time to visit them all. I needed some time to grieve on my own for my brother and my Duke.

One of my school friends also rang and wanted to meet up with me, but I have had problems in the past with listening to his complaints about the past communist era, EU and the rest. I knew the history of Slovenia and Yugoslavia much better than him and also knew how his family had allegedly greeted Hitler on his visit in 1941 and Marshall Tito in 1945! They were just like a weather vane, going with the flow.

There were many invitations from other aunties and cousins and I had to choose to see two of them. I was just too depressed about all of the sudden sad times. On the way I had to stop at the shop and bought some chocolates and sweets for the children. My two chosen aunties were living close to each other. They had fond memories of me as a young boy of fourteen who used to entertain them with my accordion. They were dancing and singing to my playing and whenever I visited them, they always used to say how much they cherished those times.

Back at the hotel I drank some of the wine which I had bought in the morning but didn't drink all of it because the next day I had to pay a visit to two more of my other aunties. They were pleased to see me after a long time. They all had grandchildren and it was nice to see their little faces light up when they saw some little presents which I had brought them from the UK. Since I had a UK sim card the phone was constantly ringing and it annoyed me and after a while I switched it off. Most of the calls were from the UK and a lot of them were from Barbara. My aunties were in their seventies and I knew that after my father's funeral, I wouldn't see them for a long time if at all. The manageress of my father's retirement home also wanted to see me before my return to the UK. She arranged a meeting at her office with my sister being present.

My sister was already there and wanted to talk to me in private before going to the manageress's office. I knew the reason. She wanted to stay in charge of father's pension account, and I contested this vehemently. At that point she became argumentative and said how, in her opinion, it was me who wanted some of the money as well. That sentence was the 'straw that broke the camel's back.' I had to keep my cool and change my tactic. I produced a business card of one of my old school friends, who had become a solicitor and said that she would be notified of my possible legal action against her for interfering with our father's pension money. She realised that I meant business. All I said then was that there was no question of me wanting any money from the pension and that I simply foresaw possible shortfalls. I just didn't want to be forced to pay any money in future years, when prices would increase to keep our father in the retirement home. His pension income would last him out. The home had a policy which also helped their occupants with a safekeeping and saving scheme. My sister just looked at me and didn't say a word. I didn't even say goodbye and left her at the table and soon after she left. It didn't even matter if she never spoke to me again. It dawned on me that she really didn't care about our father and most certainly not about me.

The manageress confirmed that I, my sister and my brother were responsible by law for looking after our father's wellbeing. She promised that she would talk to my sister and would remind her about my rights. She obviously saw straight away that it wasn't me who wanted the rest of father's pension. She even gave me a verbal forecast of how in the following four years there wouldn't be enough money from his pension and how wise my insistence was that all the pension should be paid directly into the retirement home bank account. She assured me that she would do this in a very discreet manner. But later on I learned that the manageress had done nothing of the kind and the situation with the promised rearrangements were left the same as before. I was quite frustrated. I just couldn't wait to leave Slovenia the next day.

The flight was on time and after leaving Heathrow in my car, the whole scene with my Duke's death hit me again and brought me back to the real world. The problem I had at that moment of time, was to choose- accept, in my mind, which one was a reality and which one was a dream!

I switched the phones back on and all I could see were notifications of messages upon messages. The last one was from the previous day from Barbara. It just said that she was OK and requested that I ring her upon my return. I wasn't in the mood and with a heavy heart I entered the flat and didn't even bother to unpack my suitcase. The quietness and dead silence were beginning to drive me nuts. No more of Duke's running about, no more of his jumping on my bed and certainly no more trips with him in the front basket of my bike. Although it was late, the first thing was to get rid of was my bike, sporting the basket affixed to the handlebars and I decided to do it straight away. I wheeled the bike out of my garage and I rode it for some few hundred yards and leaned it on the railings and stuck a note on the seat saying that it was free for anyone to take it away. Although it was late at night I saw two youngsters looking at it, probably reading the note and when I turned around again, the bike was gone! I felt relieved but at the same time felt a huge void.

Barbara was ringing constantly and eventually I answered the phone. She was at home and sounded cheerful possibly being glad that she was back home. She wanted to know, how the funeral and my trip went. I thought to myself what a stupid question, "how was the funeral?" There was a pause and she asked if everything was all right with me. I still didn't say anything. She said "hello, hello" and put the phone down. Since there was no urgency in her voice or any indication that she needed something, as usual I switched all the phones off.

After a while she rang me on my third phone and after answering it there was Barbara again, although I had asked her not to ring on that number, because it was for real emergencies only. I was still reeling from what had just happened in the last few days and just finished the conversation by saying that her constant spying was getting slowly 'on my tits' and the line went quiet. I had finally had enough of her silly games and literally threw my handset at the wall. I didn't care since at that time I needed to be left in peace. Even telling her about the loss of my Duke would probably end in a silly comment like 'It was only a dog.' She wasn't an animal

113

lover anyway. My mother always used to say to stay away from people who don't like flowers and animals. Barbara fitted into the category of people who didn't like animals.

I broke the promise to myself, to not drink every day and opened a bottle of gin and filled half of a tumbler and drank it in one go. I felt totally exhausted and drifted into deep sleep and woke up early due to the phone ringing. I looked around and saw that the mobile which was supposed to be ruined, was the phone that woke me up. The handset's screen was broken and therefore I couldn't see who was ringing. As soon as I answered it Barbara begged me not to put the phone down again and I listened without saying a word.

After all of her apologetic words, I told her what had happened with my Duke eight days ago. Her words of sorrow at the news of the loss of my beloved pet sounded genuine. I asked her to leave me alone for a couple days and that I would ring her then.

It was still early in the morning and when both phones were switched on again there were calls coming in "ten to the dozen." The BBC controllers wanted me to take Dr David Owen again from his home in Chelsea to the Houses of Parliament and then on to Cambridge. I had to turn it down because of my few glasses of gin and wine and they understood and appreciated my judgement. The next call was from my estate agent. He asked me when would be convenient to come to his offices because he already had a few prospective buyers. My bank manager also wanted to see me regarding my personal account which shouldn't be used as a business account. The landlord of the shop in Brick Lane was complaining about my possible breach of the lease of the flat above the shop. I shouldn't have rented it out without their permission.

None of all the calls really mattered, but deep down I knew that this nonchalant, reckless approach to a host of issues could be very costly. They had to be addressed, otherwise I would again end up in dire straits, as had happened twice before. I just needed more time. The hardest thing for me was going to be without Duke in Brick Lane on Sundays. There would be people asking me, where was my Duke. All my customers and the shop keepers knew Duke and all the neighbouring stall holders. What happened? How? Why? Who? I just imagined how difficult it was going to be to answer the same questions and give the answers over and over again. I decided not to open the shop for another 2 weeks and cover the shop rent money with my BBC earnings. There was enough work lined up for me to earn the extra money to cover the shop rent and it helped me not to be on my own for too long in the flat. Barbara was still constantly asking when I would be able to see her again and I kept postponing it till the following week.

My next job was to pick up Dawn French from her home somewhere near Waltham on Thames and take her to some 3-4 properties in Mayfair. After she had gone to see the second property, out of nowhere, there was a guy strapped with cameras who wanted to know whether I was waiting for someone. It was obvious that 'Niven car hire' controllers were at it again, meaning that they must have contacted that guy with the cameras. It also definitely confirmed what Mr Ken Livingstone once said: "How did the paparazzi know that I was coming?" I rang Dawn and told her about the photographer. Within minutes there were another two guys with cameras joining in.

Thank God Dawn didn't care and appeared through the entrance unperturbed and opened the front passenger door and we were off. She thanked me for letting her know about the photographers and gave me a £20 note. I also decided not to tell Barbara about the incident, nor any other happenings with my passengers. This discretion was paramount to me.

As usual Barbara wanted to go back to St Albans. This time it was earlier. Whilst on our way we chatted about everyday events, again, without any gossip from my side. As we approached her address she asked me to turn around and stop on the high street near the HSBC. I checked the signs for any parking restrictions and it was safe to park for an hour. She got out of the car and asked me to follow her to the Carluccio's restaurant nearby. I realised that she had already booked a table for two. Surprisingly there was no menu presented and the waiters were beginning to fill our glasses and before I knew, the first course arrived. Barbara wanted to surprise me and ordered the food that I liked. She really looked great and full of energy as if she hadn't any kind of illness at all. She talked non-stop throughout the meal. It was a different Barbara! Again, I thought of her as a very attractive woman and not as a woman with MS but as a vivacious lady. The thought about her exposing herself on the second night a good while ago suddenly became insignificant.

My two marriages and three engagements didn't make me exactly an angel. The history of my past girlfriends was probably not very different from Barbara's past boyfriends and relationships. I reminded her about the parking restriction as it was already 40 minutes over the limit. We left the restaurant and walked hand in hand towards the car. As we stopped outside her house, she produced a 'guest for one day' parking permit and stuck it to the car window.

It dawned on me that she planned the whole thing meticulously and with almost military precision. I was gob-smacked. She led me to the house and there on the dining table was a bottle of sparkling wine. She went to the kitchen and filled the wine cooler with some ice and placed the bottle into it. Wow! I was lost for words. She then went to the kitchen and served some hot toast and a cold platter of various thin sliced salamis and Gloucester cheese which is still my favourite.

6

Barbara & Her Charms

What I did next was and still is a mystery. I dialled my neighbour's number and was going to ask them to keep Duke till the next morning. My pet Duke had been by then dead for over a month and could not make out why I had just tried to ring my neighbour! I switched the phone off and asked myself if Duke wanted to warn me of something, like in the TV episodes: "The tales of the unexpected," but brushed the thought aside and filled another glass with bubbly. Barbara got hold of my hand and led me to her bedroom.

It's hard to describe in detail how and who of us two had done this, that, and other things during our lovemaking and I would leave it to the reader's imagination. For all I could say, Barbara knew how to make a man happy in this department and appeared to be insatiable. It went on for hours and I came to realise that it would be impossible to satisfy her needs and sexual requests for much longer. After all, I was working long hours and wasn't that young any more but nevertheless had to concede defeat. It wouldn't be right to divulge in some vulgar words that night's experience. Not yet. She prepared a late morning breakfast and looked at me like a cat that had got the cream. The moment my two phones were switched on, the touch screen showed unanswered calls, messages and a fax message. I checked the document and was pleased that there was a journey booked for Mr Jeffrey Archer's wife who had to be taken from her home in one of the villages up north, some 30 miles from St Albans in the afternoon.

It was an extremely well-paid job, since she would be driven from her home to Canterbury. There she would be participating in some sort of BBC live-TV debate and I was to wait for her until the end and take her back home. She was extremely nice and friendly and quite chatty. Barbara was ringing about ten times in a short space of time, but I had no time to answer her calls and hoped that it was nothing serious. Although at that time the use of a mobile phone whilst driving wasn't a serious offence, I avoided using it. It just looked more professional. I always had to work out in my head what to say to different people-passengers without sounding inquisitive. It's an art which I learned in Switzerland and thankfully, due to my knowledge of English, improved in the UK.

On our journey to Canterbury she asked me if I would take up her offer to stay at the venue and my honest reply was a no. She asked if the car was mine and I said yes, which was unusual for me to say that the expensive car was mine. There was a reason for never saying yes if somebody asked if the car belonged to me, namely passengers would on many, many occasions give me a tip if I denied that the car was mine. On a few occasions, mainly the BBC employees would try to abuse my hospitality and wanted to have their lunch in the back seat. Of course the coffee would be spilled, bits of food strewn over the car floor and on such occasions, therefore I had to make them aware that my car was still on 'plastic,' indicating that it was still on credit, although it was bought outright, and politely advised them not to eat in my car. Only on occasion when some passengers were driven on a longer journey, did the money earned warrant the cost of cleaning the car interior afterwards.

Mrs Archer, I must reiterate, wasn't inquisitive at all. I told her the story about my work as an assistant bar keeper on one of the cruise liners years before. I told her of how the crew judge which guests are most likely to leave gratuities and accordingly the chief steward would then allocate 'his mates' to those passengers.

Obviously on the understanding that the chief steward would get a 'cut'. These tricks are passed down to the next new crew on the follow up cruise. I had no chance to compete with all the goings on, after all I was a newly fledged assistant bar keeper and from the start didn't see myself lasting for long because of the strict regime. Again, the main earnings were coming from the gratuities, tips and various service charges. The overtime also helped the personnel to save some money. She was fascinated by what goes on in the background of cruise liners in general.

Stewards and all the service personnel had to have their wits about them regarding the job, or they didn't last a minute. The reason for me to quit was the rule that there is absolutely no physical contact to be made between the guests and the personnel except the handshake at the end of the cruise if even that.

It was almost 1 am when we safely arrived at her address and she gave me £30 and added an hour extra waiting time, which pushed my earnings for that day to approximately £320! I liked her manners for not enquiring about whom I had driven so far, with one exception. She remembered that I drove her husband once to their home. I am convinced the word must have gone around within the BBC that I never repeat conversations and always dress smartly. With regard to her husband, I only mentioned how he offered to park my car below his penthouse on the Southbank a while ago, whilst he entertained Clive James whom I was taking back home afterwards.

As I was about 5 miles from St Albans Barbara rang again and invited me to spend the night at her place and the next day I could take her to work. It suited me just fine because I was getting really tired. She opened her door and all she was wearing was a flimsy nighty and I nearly turned around because this wasn't what I wanted. I still entered and pretended that I didn't notice her almost see- through nightie. "Is there anything wrong?" she asked. I was embarrassed and said how badly I needed some sleep and nothing else and she should not think that I was 'hard to get' or prudish. She looked very disappointed. She then quickly went upstairs and this time came back dressed in a proper nightie, realising that I must have been very tired. We chatted a bit without mentioning anything about the previous night. She showed me her son's room which this time around looked tidy and quite cosy. I could smell a lovely scent of lavender. She gave me a kiss on my cheek and wished me good night. Immediately I checked my mobile fax machine and noticed one of the messages was from my estate agent's office and it said that they needed to see me regarding the sale of my flat the next morning. My presumption was that they, as promised, already had a buyer. I then booked a journey for Barbara to her place of work and by then it was already 3am.

Barbara knocked on my door later that morning and after breakfast we left for London. I didn't want to tell her about the sale of my flat. She was busy anyway with all the letters she had received that morning. I noticed that there was one letter which she read again and again. I didn't want to be nosy and thought if

121

she wants to tell me about it, she eventually will. She gave me a worried look. She couldn't drive and didn't understand that when she wanted to show me what it said in the letter, I wasn't going to be distracted and look at that letter whilst driving at some 65mph. I still to this day never look at my passengers whilst driving. She suggested that we stop again, where we had a disagreement on the first night we met. We managed to find a quiet corner in a coffee bar. She asked me if I could read the letter, just to confirm that she read it and understood it entirely.

The letter came from a clinic in Corfu which specialised in cases like Barbara's. She was given a date when to attend their clinic in some two months' time. Enclosed was a preliminary invoice for nearly £9000. I was surprised that there were no details of what this large amount of money would cover. I asked her if she had had dealings with that clinic before and she nodded. There were a lot of inconsistencies in the actual layout of the invoice and the letter heading didn't look professional at all. She wasn't really bothered by my remarks and after I pointed out two grammar mistakes, she just went quiet.

There was no point in discussing the matter further since she didn't ask for my advice. To be frank, I didn't even want to get involved in any financial discussion with her at that stage. I stayed at the BBC coffee bar for a while as usual, since the controllers would call me with any jobs for the rest of the day. I was privileged to be allowed to walk around the studios with impunity. There wasn't a moment that I wouldn't 'bump' into or cross paths with somebody whom I knew, or who knew me. There was no department where my access would be denied. I reminded myself how fortunate I was. I counted my lucky stars and Duke who found the drugs a few months earlier. I justifiably 'hit the roof' when I found Barbara's drugs. If caught, my life as I knew it would be in tatters in an instant.

My mobile fax machine began to bleep and there was a journey booked to go to Kingston-upon-Thames and pick up Colonel Bob Stewart, whom I drove on a few occasions. He usually talked about the then president of Yugoslavia and some of the warlords. He served time there with UNPROFOR forces. His interviews were obviously about his expert opinion of the situation in Bosnia. He was fascinated with my little stories about the hidden hate between the republics some 25 years before the actual war. I detailed some of my experiences as a tour guide in Dubrovnik from where we often took tourists on coach tours throughout the then 6 republics of Yugoslavia. It's one thing to be a tourist in any country for a short length of time, but it is another thing to understand the actual fabric of that society. Yugoslavia was an artificial state and I knew it as a very young man. It's easy now to analyse the reasons but I was born there and spoke Serbo-Croat fluently and could see the future civil war erupting 25 years before it actually happened. Mr Stewart, I hope, understood after I told him a few stories, what a lot of people in the then Yugoslavia had to go through.

As far as I was concerned, Marshal Tito, Milosevic and all the so called 'leaders, hadn't and still have none of my sympathy. I told him a story about one of the warlords, namely "Arkan." That man was a thug, a gangster and Mr Stewart obviously knew that, and he also knew the reasons why he wasn't arrested and imprisoned.

Back in 1988 Arkan was in London and was given my phone

number by an ex pupil of mine. I had actually never heard of him although most of the 'shady' characters from Yugoslavia I indeed knew through my small driving school. Some of my pupils who were of Serbian descent would sometimes tell me stories about most of them. As he came to my little office and introduced himself, I took an instant dislike to him. His demeanour made me uncomfortable with all those blingy gold chains around his neck and on both of his wrists. He said quietly: "I am in a hurry to get a UK driving licence." I asked him how quick and he mentioned in 2-3 days. "That's impossible and there is no way you could get a UK licence not even in a month, Mr Arkan!"

He paused for a moment and produced a wad of £50 notes. "Look, Mr Arkan, I have been in this country for many years now and I presume that what you are asking me to do would be a criminal offence. And for some paltry £300-400 pounds I would lose my D.O.T instructor's licence and in all probability end up in prison." I went on to say: "I can give you all the forms you'll need to apply for your provisional licence and then the application for your driving test." Whilst I was gathering up all the forms, he began to demand that I should fill out all the forms and that he would be back in two days to collect his new UK driving licence. I picked up the phone and speedily dialled 999. He realised that he had misjudged how I operated my small business. He then pointed his fore finger at me, akin to what gangsters do in the movies and ran off. Later on, I learned even more about his crimes which were 'as long as his arm.' One of the Serbs who lived nearby told me that he heard the whole story and how Arkan talked about me and described me as some crazy man and a tough cookie. The very same man, Arkan,

later on became a leader of the Serbian National Guard called "The Tigers" and was subsequently killed.

Whilst waiting for Mr Stewart, Barbara kept asking me over the phone what she should do with that letter about her forthcoming appointment in Corfu. "You should ignore it and bin it," I replied and pointed out all the spelling mistakes in their logo which looked too amateurish. It was too soon for me to get involved with Barbara's financial affairs. At the end of our conversation she asked if I would like to drive her back home at the end of her shift. I was still very tired and besides, the next day was the date to sign the exchange of contracts and I had to turn her down but promised to drive her on her next working day. I had to finish our conversation because Mr Stewart walked into the huge BBC lobby and was looking around for me. The journey back to his place was reasonably quick and by 10pm I was home.

As soon as I walked through my door there were phones ringing again. Both numbers were unknown to me. I answered the first one and it was a German newscaster whom I drove around London a while ago. He wanted me to be his and his entourage's PA for 3-4 days whilst in London. Apparently, they came in their own car, but couldn't manage the London traffic. Klauss asked me to meet them at the BBC the next morning but I had to turn it down.

I offered to see them in the afternoon after explaining the reason why the morning was 'out.' I had a moral obligation to go to the estate agency and tell the agents that the sale of my place should be postponed to a later date.

Klauss and his three companions were already waiting for me at the BBC and were pleased to see me. They were four employees of

Deutsche Rundfunk and needed someone who spoke German and knew London and the surrounding counties well. My task would be to drive them to the places they wanted to go to. I would also arrange their bookings for lunches and dinners for the duration of three days. We discussed for a while where they wanted to go, where they would want to eat and if they intended to go to one of the theatres. I suggested that they write down everything we had discussed and I thanked them for trusting me.

Klauss just said that he knew the only man who could do all this was me. Obviously, he remembered that I drove him a while ago and how I had mentioned my work as a tour guide in Dubrovnik. Most of the procedures with regard to travel arrangements were very familiar to me anyway. And the most important question was if their car insurance policy did cover any driver beside him. Finally, the question popped up how much I would charge them for doing this.

I didn't have to inform the BBC of this private arrangement because it wouldn't be with my car and there was no conflict of interests, since the BBC had no such services to offer. "I have to see the itinerary and we'll work something out so that both parties will be satisfied." With that said I still insisted on some kind of plan-itinerary. When asked when they needed my 'service,' they all said in almost one voice: "Now!" I burst out laughing and told them: "impossible," as it was too soon and told them straight away that I was definitely going to do the tour but we would need to go into more details of the myriad places and restaurants they wanted to go to. They had taken into consideration all the parking charges, all the possible paid reservations, theatre booking fees and a whole

host of extras if needed. I suggested that if they trusted me, they should organise a cash card which could be bought over the counter at any Thomas Cook exchange offices. Alternatively, they could leave me whichever cash card they were able to organise, so that I would manage and pay all expenses. I gave them a quick scenario: "Let's say you would all like to have a lunch in Windsor but we were still driving. I would make a call to the restaurant which I knew and send them a fax with your credit card details. It would be much quicker, since according to you, time is of the essence."

I also stressed that use of my own credit card would interfere with my tax returns. There was no other way, but to tell them straight, that if they didn't trust my integrity, there was no point in doing anything at all. They looked at each other and said: "Verstanden," which in German means 'understood' and we ended up laughing.

Klauss seemed to understand that I knew what I was talking about and that my approach was the correct one. I just didn't want us to end up like headless chickens and also didn't want to tour around London and neighbouring counties for more than 4 days. I had to think about my shop, which was closed during the week except on Sundays. I added that they should fax me all that we had discussed that evening and I would give them the price.

It was an hour later when Klauss faxed some three pages with all the points of interest. All the places and some of the restaurants were known to me, but we would need more than ten days to do all that. I rang Klauss and we were talking for a good while and came to an agreement that for the 4 days of 12 hours work my charge would be in the region of £1000. Klauss even offered more but I

told him about the progress of the book I was writing and maybe one day he instead could put me in touch with one of the German publishers as my bonus for taking care of them whilst in the UK. Unfortunately he was not able to organise a cash card since he wasn't a UK resident and ended our conversation by saying that I would use their company's credit card. We arranged that I would see them the next morning at 7 am at BBC reception. I asked Klauss to leave their car in the BBC car park until my arrival so that I could leave my car at the same spot where their car was.

Whilst talking to Klauss, Barbara's calls showed up every 20 minutes and eventually I answered her call. After telling her about my forthcoming venture which would last for 4 days, she sounded a bit disappointed that we weren't going to see each other for almost a week.

It was around 6am and Klauss was ringing me just to make sure that everything was okay and that they would meet me at the BBC main reception in about an hour. I had worked as an assistant concierge in Switzerland and knew about German punctuality. I had the same approach and I was at the main reception 20 minutes early, but they were all already waiting for my arrival.

Klauss's face lit up as soon as he saw me. They were amazed how big the TV centre was. Now in 2020 after a total refurbishment it's even bigger. We sat down in the cafeteria and on the back of typed pages I pointed out all the distances to the places they would like to see. It took me a while back at home to draw a rough map of London and encircle it within a 60 miles radius. Then I divided the encompassed M25 area into four quarters. Obviously, we would start at the north of the Thames and possibly towards the

west towards Heathrow. There was Windsor, Eton, the Windsor Safari Park and Oxford. Luckily, I had already been to Magdalen College, Oxford, before and knew exactly how to get there. "This is about all what we would be able to see for today" and they nodded as if to say we are in agreement. "We must travel in a westerly direction because the notorious rush hour traffic flows in an easterly direction towards London" and they nodded again. I thought to myself: "so far so good." They had the same type of car and it took me only a few moments to adjust all the mirrors and check the lights and the brakes. Klauss commented about my almost new Mercedes and how glad he was to see me making progress in my life. There were two ladies and another gentleman in the group. I was really pleased that they fully trusted my driving, after we joined the already busy motorway. Klauss was telling his companions how they should relax and enjoy the ride, because he knew that as a UK driving instructor, I sat in the left seat whilst teaching.

I took the whole thing as a new adventure and immediately began to enjoy it. We went to Windsor Castle first and the weather was beautiful. We found a space to park just a few yards away from the main entrance. Now, in 2020 it would be impossible to park anywhere close to the entrance.

When we approached the entrance, the usher let us through the gate without an extensive body search and was very courteous. It was only when we walked around for a while, that I noticed the BBC official badge was still dangling around my neck. Inadvertently I had forgotten to take my official BBC name tag off and that was the reason for the 'little special treatment' by the security.

It wasn't against the law to wear my name tag, but it would be an offence to use my BBC badge to gain entrance to the castle, for example. I wasn't asked if we were from the BBC on an official visit and therefore wasn't worried too much. Klauss and Helga, Gert and Trudy wore their DR (Deutsche Rundfunk) badges as well. The whole tour would last about 2 hours, but I left them after 20 minutes. They knew the reason straight away and appreciated my diplomacy hence they also needed some privacy. I knew that they would want to talk to each other in private without my presence. "Klauss, you have my mobile number. Give me a call 15 minutes before you'll plan to come out" was my short comment, "and I will turn the car around and wait for you, close to the entrance".

My advice was also taken on board for them not to take any professional cameras with them as they wouldn't be allowed to film without prior permission. I had enough time to walk around outside the castle, treading the old little and narrow cobbled streets. It was time to give Barbara a call back after noticing she had rung a few times during the morning. She sounded more cheerful and wanted to know if I was enjoying my new adventure.

"Yes and I needed something like this type of work, just the change from the everyday routine, and I am glad that those reporters have chosen me to help them out." Barbara agreed and after chatting for a while she wanted to know when I would see her again. I told her that this coming Sunday at my shop would be a good idea and rang off. I went back to the car to check the parking meter and inserted further coins just to be sure that the car wouldn't be clamped or towed away and after a short while made myself comfortable in the car. I obviously didn't want to

touch any of my guests' stuff and saw that they trusted me fully and unreservedly. All their paperwork was laid bare on the back seat as were their passports.

After a while I was racking my brain trying to remember any restaurants on our route to Oxford. I just remembered that a while ago one of my jobs was to drive Mr Johnson, the former Mayor of London and now the Prime Minister, to a nice restaurant not far from Oxford town centre. Maybe my guests would like to have lunch after their tour of Magdalen College. But if they wanted to go to Eton College after seeing Windsor Castle, then they could have a lunch somewhere in Eton. The time went by fast and once we were ready to leave Windsor, I pointed out that there wouldn't be enough time to see all three planned places and have a lunch as well in one day.

Whilst driving towards Eton I told them a true story about some aggressive chimpanzee habits in the safari park. "I was following the cars in front of me. Suddenly one of the chimpanzees jumped on my car roof and then climbed down onto the bonnet and wanted to rip my windscreen out of the window frame. I accelerated briefly, and the chimp fell off, but the damage was already done with a windscreen wiper slightly twisted." Klauss was glad that I told them about it and thus no Windsor Safari Park. So far so good with the itinerary and in no time we were in Eton. They had all the paperwork ready and the permission to film on Eton College's grounds. Klauss gave me his mobile phone, which apparently the Germans call "the handy" and asked to call Magdalen College in Oxford and tell them the approximate time of our arrival. According to my calculations by the time they had finished in

Eton, with what they intended to do, there would be no students present.

Klauss had all the paperwork and permission to film the graduating students and professors as well. I had some 3 hours spare time, although it was my third trip to the college, therefore I wasn't excited any more but it was still nice to see all the graduates in their robes. I walked towards the little village centre and stopped at a pub. I ordered a coffee and rang Magdalen College. They weren't very pleased about the Klauss's time schedule but nevertheless agreed to wait for us. I rang Helga and explained the situation about the college's comments and that there was nothing to worry about.

I had enough time to ring Barbara again and she told me, after a lengthy conversation, of her son's forthcoming visit. She said how he would like to meet me whilst visiting her. I suggested that they both come on the coming Sunday to my shop. She didn't mention anything further about her appointment in Corfu and I wasn't going to enquire about her plans in that matter either.

It was about 6pm when we reached Oxford. Klauss was in good spirits and thankfully I knew most of the short cuts which saved us over an hour. Even Oxford had a rush hour! The Dean of the College was already waiting outside the entrance. After greeting each other my guests took all their equipment through those huge arches over two centuries old oak doors and disappeared. It took them over an hour to appear again, seemingly happy and we were on the road again, heading for London. They were by then exhausted but were still talking to each other in German and complimented Klauss for finding someone who knew 'the ropes.' It might appear that I sounded or was somehow conceited, or 'a Mr know it all.' Maybe a bit of self- congratulatory but this is unfounded as you'll realise in the following chapters. My work within the BBC was based on recommendations and all I wanted was to be as near perfect as possible.

Klauss asked if I knew any good restaurants in the vicinity. "It all depends on what type of restaurant you are looking for. For example we have just passed a well- known steak house in Marlow and you will like it," I replied and asked if they wanted to see it first and then decide whether to stay or not. They all agreed. I didn't tell them how and whom I drove to that particular restaurant. I thought if the restaurant was good for Boris Johnson, it'll surely be good enough for them. I had met the manager before and when he heard my name, 'hey presto' the table was reserved. They instantly liked the restaurant.

Whilst they were eating, I went for a walk and checked all the messages and looked for any missed calls. I paid with Klauss's credit card as suggested and it all went without a glitch. It was nearly 11pm when we returned to the BBC car park. They were extremely happy at how the day had passed without any problems. He wanted me to use his car to drive home since it would be much quicker to set off the next morning. I turned it down because of a possible accident and things could have become complicated, especially with a foreign registered car and without any car insurance details or paperwork.

At any moment I expected a call from Barbara. It was her third call of that day and I answered it. It was rather late I and was hoping that our conversation wasn't going to be long as I was getting tired.

She asked me if I was anywhere near the BBC studios. "Nope" I answered and asked her to ring me back later on. The line was bad, and it appeared that she was somewhere outdoors. I wanted to surprise her and turned my car around and drove straight back towards the studios. I drove slowly towards the main entrance and saw Barbara going into a car which was about 100 yards down the road. But the car wasn't a private hire car since it had no TFL sticker on the rear windscreen which would indicate that the car was licensed by TFL (Transport for London). I decided to follow the car. The driver must have known the route since it was the shortest way to the M1.

I had only the side lights on and was using all my skills to avoid them thinking they were being followed. After a few miles I allowed one car to be in front of me just to make sure that Barbara's driver did not realise that they were being followed. Just before reaching the M1 the driver turned into a narrow road. It was a dead - end road. I stopped in the small gap between two cars, turned the lights off and followed the car on foot. From the driver's brake lights, I could see that it turned into a college car park. I was anxious to see what Barbara was up to. I didn't want to go too close, therefore I went behind some small bushes and waited. By then, in my mind, it was obvious that Barbara was back to her old tricks as I originally guessed when she flaunted her legs and breasts to me nearly 8 months ago.

I just imagined her 'riding' the driver with the same vigour as with me. I wasn't jealous at all, only sad that it was all lies that she kept telling me. It was nearly 1 am and Barbara was in the car for nearly 10 minutes. Surprisingly there weren't any noises coming from the interior, although by now I was only 2-3 feet away. No squeaking came from the car either which would prove my presumption that they were 'busy'! I just stood there and listened. By then I knew that I wouldn't be able to drive Klauss the next morning because I wouldn't have had enough sleep.

I was already planning how to cancel the next day and somehow persuade him to wait until the next day. I was at risk of losing a nice little earner. A few more minutes passed and I asked myself "If I lose all that money, so what?" I was at the point of no return. Determined to find out what kind of a woman I was going out with, the money suddenly didn't matter any more. The most important thing to me was to catch Barbara cheating on me, despite her constant calls and sweet words about wanting to be only with me and with all her pretentious show of love. All of a sudden both of my phones went off almost simultaneously. I bit my lips and all of the car interior lights came on and I expected to see Barbara undressed - naked - and in a sexual position of some kind. Nothing like it. Instead out of the driver seat climbed a woman!

Barbara by then recognised me and her hand, clutching a small parcel, quickly disappeared in her handbag. I was pleasantly surprised at how wrong I was. I was glad that I was spared my partner betraying my trust. I wanted to say something but wasn't able to say anything. The words just simply didn't come out of my mouth. I just stood there and looked sheepishly at that woman and Barbara whilst she too was climbing out of her back seat. There was nothing to indicate that she was engaged in any sexual activity whatsoever. My brain was in overdrive and I speedily composed myself and began to realise that there was another reason why

Barbara was in that car.

The only other reason why Barbara was in that private car in the car park, in my mind, must have been the cannabis! She asked the woman to bear with her for a moment. She pulled me to one side and asked me in a husky voice what the hell was I doing there. "You shouldn't spy on me!" I was quick with a reply: "You have a cheek to say that" and went on: "Now we are quits. You were spying and going through my PC files to see what was in them and now I wanted to see what you were up to!"

I expected a barrage of swear words any moment but instead all she said was "Would you take me home please and we'll discuss it all then." "Not on your nelly because I can only imagine what you and this lady were doing" was my reply. "There was nothing sexual going on between us, if you are implying that there was." "Yes, I know that now Barbara and that is what worries me. It's the cannabis, isn't it? And if it is, I am not driving you home in any circumstances because you have not taken on board what we discussed when you left your little carrier bag filled with cannabis back at my place. Most probably that package which you swiftly put into your bag is filled with the same stuff."

I kept on questioning her relentlessly. "Do you know what you are doing? Do you know who these people are that are bringing and selling all this stuff? You even meet them right under the BBC's nose. Do you realise that the dealers are recruiting you to be their mule to bring the drugs into the BBC premises?", and at the end, I added "I can't see your eyes right now but am in no doubt that you are already doped up."

I decided at that point not to swear at her, since in my mind, in the end it would only be her who would suffer and walked towards my car, started the engine and left Barbara where she was. I had no remorse, nor did I feel sorry for her. I feared for my own safety because I knew that if she was caught, the police might come to question me as well.

But something in my mind told me to stop and reverse my car into the road where I stopped a few minutes ago. Barbara was still standing next to that car and seemingly arguing with the woman driver. She looked surprised and pleased at the same time to see that I had come back. I asked her if she definitely had no drugs of any sort on her. Through her tears she assured me that I had got it all terribly wrong this time. "All right then, say good bye to your lady driver and I'll take you home." The woman driver looked at me angrily and didn't say a word. I could see that Barbara hesitated and maybe she thought that my sudden change of mind about driving her home after all the things said in the last 20 minutes was some kind of prelude to more questioning or a bad joke.

As soon as we reached the M1 my mobile rang and I asked Barbara to answer it, since I rarely use my mobile whilst driving. It was Klauss. I asked her to tell him that I'd ring him back as soon as possible.

Ironically, by then we were approaching the service station, and passing the very spot where I changed the wheel with a punctured tyre almost a year ago. "Let's go and have a coffee Zinco and I'll buy it." I actually wanted to stop there anyway, so that we could discuss things on neutral ground, where I could say what I wanted without being under possible threat of being thrown out of her house.

Whilst she went to get us our drinks I knew that there must be something urgent, hence that late night call. Klauss was ringing again and started to apologise profoundly, saying that they had to return to Germany in 2 hours' time. He wanted to know how much they owed me and that the envelope with cash would be waiting for me at the main reception.

He continued to say that they would be back in a week's time and would appreciate if I was prepared to drive them again. "Of course I will" and I assured him that there was no need to leave any money. "By the way, Zinco, you can keep the credit card until we come back." "Your credit card, Klauss, is in the glove compartment and I forgot to tell you" and just reiterated again that they should simply ring me a day or so beforehand. "Zinco, the way you organised the whole thing so far is unbelievable!" I was gob-smacked by him trusting me with his credit card. Luckily enough, Barbara couldn't hear the last sentence. I, on the other hand, thought how strange and weird Klauss's comment sounded. If he only knew on how many occasions I was not the sharpest tool in the box'!

He hadn't had a clue that an hour earlier I was just about to ask him to put the following day's work on hold till the next day. Barbara brought me a strong coffee and we sat down. Her eyes were all red and I guessed by the look on her face, she was expecting another 'question time.'

I said nothing for a while and wanted her in her own time to tell me about the late night meeting with a woman driver. It was very unusual of Barbara not to say a word for a good while. Eventually she opened her bag and produced a largish envelope. "What's this?" I asked and she invited me to open it.

There was a video cassette and a CD labelled 'Barbara's audition'. "See, it wasn't drugs I put into my bag after all. This is a video of me doing an audition at the modelling agency in West London a while ago. Andy originally booked it for me without telling me. M&S were looking for a new and 'fresh face advertising and promoting their women's lingerie and underwear." "Jane is the driver's name and she supposedly had a prepared contract for me to sign, but the money wasn't right. I can earn more by doing overtime and night work which pays double. Whilst discussing all this with Jane, your phone rang." I explained to Barbara that I simply wanted to see where and who she was going with, that is all. It wasn't an act of jealousy but the thought of her being unfaithful that made me consider following her in the car.

"I was protecting my interests and am prepared to take you home without charging you any money for doing so. You are at liberty once we reach your house to say goodbye and I will move on." "Please," Barbara said, "don't do that. Why can't you stay overnight at my place? I have to book a car anyway to get to work later on this morning." "By the way, you will be paid for this journey as well." I thought this is typical Barbara. Predictably unpredictable! I didn't say anything for a short while and wanted her to become more comfortable. She went on: "Zinco, I have contacted my doctor and have enquired about getting marijuana on prescription. The only problem with that would be the disclosure clause of drug dependence whilst working for the Corporation. I read their policy through and it does stipulate that their employees are compelled to reveal any dependencies, whether it be drugs, alcohol and so on. It would be on my doctor's records and the company might demote me to a lower position and subsequently lower pay or even dismiss me." "At least you see that I was rightfully overprotecting myself by not getting involved with any drug dependent person. I would suggest that you talk to your Trade Union. Unfortunately, whoever you'll be talking to and seeking advice from on this issue, it will always go on a record of some sort. I genuinely feel sorry for you and have no answer nor any easy solution to give you, perhaps you should try to explore the option of freelancing for them?" I advised. "Yes, Zinco, I think that would be a good idea and it's well worth exploring it, but it would be make me financially very insecure and only God knows how many more years I have left before my MS progresses further." I decided to change the subject just to ease the pressure and duress we had both been through in the last hour and a half.

"Will I be able to see what's on the CD and video tape?" "Yes, if you wish to you can watch it tonight." I felt tired and suggested we continue our journey towards St Albans.

Once indoors she went straight to the kitchen and came back with a bottle of red wine. Although she didn't drink I could see from the label that it was a very expensive wine. I asked her at what time she was going to work. "Don't worry, I can change my shift and we would have the rest of the night and the whole day to ourselves." I didn't have to think twice about what she had in mind and opened the bottle, poured some of the wine in a larger than normal glass. She disappeared again for a while and called from the top of stairs, asking me to go to the bedroom because there was something for me. I entered the bedroom and saw a new men's suit half unwrapped on the bed. A new pair of shoes, still boxed, were next to a men's shirt. I looked at the label and it was a very expensive Saville Row shirt. "Barbara, is this some kind of 'send-off' present"? I said loudly in a joking voice "and how much will this cost me in the long run?"

The words 'How much will this cost me in the long run' will also haunt me forever. I made my way back to the living room where Barbara was fiddling with her video player, and she asked me to help to make it work.

It only took me seconds to see that it wasn't in a 'Play' mode. Although she held an important job at the BBC and knew how to operate their software programs etc, she obviously hadn't got round to learning about setting up her own wi-fi, laptop and mobiles. Her lack of knowledge of operating her household appliances, gave me cause of concern.

She, as mentioned already, once forgot to turn off her gas cooker and couldn't get my cooker working a while ago. Obviously, in my mind her MS caused this. Whilst having another glass of wine, we watched the video of her putting on all sorts of Marks and Spencer's own brand lingerie, dresses, underwear and other clothes. She looked fabulous. I congratulated her and kissed her on her cheek and asked her if she had forgiven me for accusing her and the lady driver of being involved in some kind of a drug deal about 2 hours ago. She did but felt sorry for Jane who had offered her a possible new career although she had turned the offer down. Surprisingly she then got herself a glass and filled it with wine. "To hell with all the medication, I want to get drunk!" "But Barbara, don't you think that it could be harmful if your medication prohibits you to consume any alcohol?". "Yes I know, Zinco but today I haven't taken any and tonight nothing will stop me from having a good drink." With that she went upstairs to her bedroom and to the kitchen and came back to the dining room with another already opened bottle. She took my glass and filled it with the fresh wine she had just fetched from the kitchen. Only then I noticed her skimpy dress with her 'inviting' look. I had to go to relieve myself and when I returned I noticed that she had already emptied her glass. To this day I can't remember from which bottle she was filling her glass. After my third glass I didn't feel as tired as before. We ended up in bed, but I knew there was something added to the wine. Much later, Barbara confessed that she added a Viagra to my wine. No wonder I felt reinvigorated.

I finally crashed out and slept for more than 10 hours and woke up still exhausted. Barbara changed her shift to work overnight and all that was left for me to do was to take her to the studios later that evening. My controllers knew about my 2 days off, but they still kept sending me faxes with jobs available, and luckily, they knew my working pattern. But if there was an 'emergency' or 'special' job or journey to be carried out, they were confident that I would help them out.

From that night's experience with my 'insatiable Barbara', the seeds were sewn to the countdown of events and a disastrous end had begun!

When back in my own home, there was a lot of mail. I started with the first one, which came from my estate agent. It was about a cash buyer for my flat. The offer was for £210.000 with the caveat that the contracts were to be exchanged before 10 days were up, starting from the date when the letter-offer was posted.

I owed some £65,000 to the building society and there was another small loan to be repaid. I had an overdraft for £15,000 and after a quick calculation there was going to be a lot of money left. I reckoned that after all the money owed and the final purchase payment for the property to the Council at a heavily discounted price, I would be some £120,000 better off. I would move to one of the flats above the shop in Brick Lane and would be ready to look for a small house somewhere in London suburbia. The plan to go to the US was put on hold again. There was so much to be done and on top of it all, I was at any moment expecting a phone call from my sister or neighbour, to inform me of my father's passing. I shut all my windows and went to my bedroom and sat on my bed in total darkness. In my mind I went over all the possible things that could possibly go wrong with the sale of my flat. With the sale, I was to lose the use of my two garages below the flat.

With my move to live in Brick Lane, I would be too far to accept any jobs at short notice because of the time needed to travel the distance between the East and the West End. There was a danger that my expensive car would be open to vandalism if parked on the street. My short shop lease also came to my mind and I had to take into account, the possibility of the landlord increasing the rent to an extortionate level.

There was also the possibility that I would change my mind and still pursue my ambition to go to the US after my father's funeral. But where would I go if things didn't go to plan and the extension of my lease on the shop and two flats above wasn't successful? After a long talk to myself, literally, and repeating over again the proverb: 'Why repair a vase if it isn't broken?' I at that moment in time found it easier to speak out loud about my thoughts and it wasn't the first time I had done that. And I went on: "Zinco, your beloved Duke is in a better place now and although you still think of him every day you will overcome the grief in time. Duke wouldn't want to see you making a mistake in your life, because he was taken away from you and you miss him terribly."

It was my mobile ringing that interrupted all these thoughts and talking to myself. I could see it was Barbara and she just wanted to know that I was alright. I didn't want to divulge my plans in any conversation, at least not at that time. Another hour went by and I decided after much thought not to sell my flat as of yet. After a few hours rest, I rang my estate agent and told him the reason for putting the sale on hold. He took it all on board and agreed that the sale would have been done too hastily. I promised that the sale would eventually happen and that they would be the sole agents.

Then it was back to the normal daily routine. Clive James wanted me to take him home from The West End to Rotherhithe. Peter Bazalgette needed to catch his flight from Gatwick airport and Katie Adie had to be taken to Buckingham Palace to deliver a portrait-painting of HM the Queen. The very witty Maureen Lipman had to be driven to Elstree studios. And there was Sacha Distell whom I had a job to calm down, because my controllers got the time wrong, but nevertheless after I showed him my fax with the wrong time, he apologised and offered me a free ticket for one of his concerts.

At the age of 15, my school promoted a periodical, translated half way from English to Slovenian and written by famous astrophysicist Patrick Moore and I signed up for it. It was fascinating to read about all the advancing technologies and so many decades later, I drove Patrick Moore twice in succession to Cambridge. He was bemused by my remarks about how I had read many of his publications. On my second journey, whilst driving him home, I wanted to ask him something about the moon landing. On my first journey I revealed how my father almost forced me to spend a lot of time in a 'dark room' to develop black and white film rolls and photos. Now, this time I plucked up the courage and asked one question: "Who was filming and taking the photos from the distances shown, because there would have to be a long pole fixed to the moon lander in order to get all that landing in focus?" He looked at me, smiled and said: "I don't have an answer for that" and we changed the subject and I was really glad that he hadn't taken my question seriously. But deep down he must have realised that I knew a lot about photography and the angles, focusing, exposure etc. By the way, I am not promoting any conspiracies, and these are only my thoughts.

A few months passed and I was offered a job to accompany a team from RAI (Italian state television) to go to Glasgow to be their assistant for a few days. My task would entail organising their stay in Glasgow, their dinners, in short, all things I was familiar with. Barbara all of a sudden stopped calling me. After a few attempts to contact her I gave up and waited for her to call me instead.

After my return from Scotland, there weren't any missed calls shown on my mobile and I decided to call her son in Durham. He was quite surprised to hear my voice and in a laid back way, said that I shouldn't worry. "Zinco, she went to Ireland and rest assured she is doing fine," "Andrew, I was only concerned about your mother's well- being and it was only for her sake. You should be glad that I rang you!" I sensed that he wasn't even going to say thank you for being concerned about my mum. It was fine by me but I concluded that his voice sounded a bit sarcastic. I took it that he was trying to belittle me or at least downplaying my effort of inquiring about his mum. I just couldn't resist saying: "Andrew, are you by any chance thinking that I was checking on your mum?" I was ready for a verbal showdown with him right there and then. All Andrew said after my last sentence was 'sorry' and rang off.

My gut feeling about Andrew's attitude towards me from then on was confirmed. I wanted to find out the reason for his bad behaviour and total lack of respect towards me. I somehow worked out that most probably behind Andrew's hostile and sarcastic way of talking to me was Barbara. Maybe she didn't want me to create a bond with her son. At that point I quite frankly didn't give a 'hoot' about him! If that was how Barbara's son was going to behave towards me, I was ready to walk away. I had already walked away from this dysfunctional relationship three times.

About two months passed and I had quite happily immersed myself in my work and hadn't bothered to ring any of Barbara's numbers.

Noel Edmunds became my regular customer. At the time, he was buying a horse for his wife, but it was an unusual breed. There is a small town in Slovenia called Lipica, where they breed, rear and train famous Lippizaner dressage horses and they are black at birth. I gathered a lot of information about his planned flight by his helicopter to Lipica from the UK. My past flying experience helped me to find out about various aviation regulations in Slovenia.

Once, while driving him to his heliport in Battersea, he told his guests, how I had helped him to buy that horse.

About a month later, he asked me to drive one of his own chauffeurs or assistants with my car to London's East End. I had some 20 minutes spare time and sipped my coffee on one of the BBC benches. The actual forecourt was a few feet below where I sat. I could hear someone shouting some obscenities over the phone to someone at the other end. I could clearly hear Noel's and his wife's name mentioned and it went on for a good while. As I was about to phone Noel, the man who sat in the Bentley car got out and headed to the reception area. I ran after him and asked if it was him to be driven to the East End. "Yes," he replied and added, "And you must be Zinco." We drove for about 2 hours around the East End and made various stops. Most of the time he was on the phone and again I presumed, Noel's wife's name was mentioned many times.

After a few weeks I picked up Noel again from Battersea heliport and noticed that this time he was alone. In the following months, I finally heard that he was in the middle of a divorce. I found out, that the man I drove around the East End a while before, was presumably his wife's lover! I never dared to contact Noel to tell him about that man's rude language while presumably talking to his wife some months earlier.

The shop was doing fine and I had managed to extend the lease for a further 3 years with only a slight rent increase. Since Barbara hadn't called, I realised that I could live quite happily without her and hoped my life was back to normal. No more silly conversations with her. No more constant interruption of my sleep with her calls.

In short, I felt that a big burden had just fallen off my shoulders. My estate agents were constantly keeping me up with new offers and I was again tempted to go ahead with the sale of my maisonette. At the same time, I was looking at some small properties in North London under the scheme 'buy to rent.'

My idea was to sell the flat, take up another mortgage and let the new property out. I would stay in one of the flats above my shop in Brick Lane. The only problem would be to find a secure garage or a private parking space nearby and the arduous journey to my base of operations in West London-BBC studios in Wood Lane. I signed the exchange of contracts, despite my accountant's advice not to. I still remember his words ringing in my ears: "Don't do it, at least not just yet!" Well there was no way back. It took me nearly 2 weeks to move and empty my flat including a lot of clutter which was later sold outside my shop. I found secure parking as well and felt contended with what I had done. During all this time I wasn't able to do much work for either car hire companies and they were waiting patiently for me to return. The proceeds of the sale were safely deposited at my bank.

7

Meeting Elaine Stritch - The Actress

Elaine Stritch was an American actress in the 'Two's Company' TV series and that year, she was living at the famous Savoy Hotel. She was here in the UK to appear on the Royal Variety Show in West London and I had driven her from the BBC studios back to her hotel. Somehow, during the journey, I cracked a joke about something, and she found me quite funny and we 'clicked' in an instant. She had an account with the second cab company I had a contract with, and she wanted to ensure that for the duration of her stay in London, I was to be her driver. Unfortunately, the controllers weren't happy with her request, because they needed me to also cover other jobs. She then contacted BBC transport and the manager had no objection to letting me stay with her as long as she needed. Obviously, other drivers were a bit jealous and tried to 'snatch-poach' her journeys from me, so some of the drivers would wait for her, without my knowledge, at the Savoy Hotel. Elaine sussed it out straight away and would ring me and remind me that she was still waiting for my arrival. On one other occasion, she shouted at the Savoy porters, because they were allowing the drivers with their Rolls-Royces and luxury 'Maibach limousines to park right next to the hotel entrance and try to entice her to be driven in their cars! She even took me to see some of her friends in their apartments near Harrods. Within the period of 12 days, I was doing her shopping, I would accompany her to some of the most expensive restaurants, like Claridge's, (no we didn't dine together,) and also do some of her bank errands, in short, I sensed that she was expecting me to join her in the USA as her PA. There was nothing intimate going on between us two. She even nudged me to meet and talk to some ladies of my age. To this day, I still can't understand why I didn't take up her offer to join her in to the States. Maybe it was all down to my independence here in the UK, maybe at the time I still had some feelings for Barbara. I had a good life here in the UK, and with me going to the USA, at my age, and becoming dependent on Elaine just didn't appeal to me. I sent her a few emails afterwards which she acknowledged and asked if I had changed my mind about her offer and she would take me on as her PA immediately. All her expensive presents were also later on stolen by Barbara.

It was by now over 2 months since Barbara's sudden disappearance. Then on my next Sunday trading day, there was Barbara standing outside the shop's closed door! It must have been about 7am and I was gob-smacked. I had no choice but to let her in.

All I could say was how surprised I was to see her and ask her the reason for coming to see me. She was surprised at my nonchalant approach to her question, whether I missed her. I gave her my honest answer and simply said "NO!" I had a small kitchenette but hadn't managed to get anything into the fridge except a carton of milk. There was virtually no need for me to cook amidst dozens of take-away restaurants. Besides there was the BBC restaurant where I could eat at any time. I suggested that she got us some hot bagels with salmon and a coffee or tea. I handed her a £10 note, which she refused to take and off she went.

While she was away, I noticed that she hadn't left her bag behind, a sure sign of the fact that someone didn't trust me but it didn't really bother me.

8

Barbara's Pregnancy, Revelations & Lies

I kept asking myself what should I do? I decided to wait and see what she had to say about herself and her absence. I had to open the shop and set up two stalls outside as usual and by the time she was back, there were people already milling around my stalls.

I brought out two chairs and we both tucked into our bagels. She didn't say a word about her time in Ireland and I certainly wasn't going to question her, because as far as I was concerned, the questionable relationship we had, was over. She insisted on helping me and in my mind, there was nothing to lose with her doing that. My other two helpers turned up and we got as much stuff as possible out of the shop because the weather was gorgeous. Barbara kept constantly looking towards the end of the road as if she was expecting someone. What I wasn't going to allow in any circumstances, was her bringing someone along with her and especially unannounced. If there was someone coming along and joining her in my presence, I knew that it would make my blood boil and I would send her and, whoever she was waiting for, packing! As I served a customer, my eyes caught glimpse of Barbara's son Andrew walking down the road towards the shop. She asked him to say hello and to apologise to me for his standoffish stance during our last conversation two months ago.

I was surprised but at the same time baffled by the sudden friendly reception and told Andrew to forget about the previous encounter. He asked if he could be of any help and I replied: "Yes, keep an eye on the crystals and call me to price the items and let me deal with the money." He seemed to be fascinated by all the different colours shining from hundreds of glittering chandelier pieces exposed to the direct sunlight. The time was flying and the rush was over at about 1pm. It didn't take long to cart all the stuff back into the shop. All I had to do was to watch that the right pieces of furniture and some statues were in the right place since it would be left to just me to take them out the next Sunday. I paid Jack and Rooney their well-earned money and a 'fiver' on top. They were very reliable and honest and I wanted to keep them happy. The time came to offer Barbara £20 and another £10 to Andrew but they refused to take it.

I then repeated, that there was nothing in my fridge to offer them and asked who had driven them to the shop. "We came by train and the underground and wanted to invite you to my house to have dinner with us two. Andrew has learned how to cook a leg of lamb Greek style in a slow cooker and by the time we arrive it will be ready. All that is needed are the roast potatoes which Andrew will buy at a Greek restaurant in Wood Green when we are on our way." With that she asked if I was hungry and would I accept their invitation and added that I should stay overnight at her place as there would be a nice little earner waiting for me the next day. "I have to go to Stoke Mandeville hospital to get some results regarding my MS and then you could take me to the BBC studios. It's a well-paid job and I hope you will accept my offer." I just said OK and went to get dressed but she insisted I just come dressed as I was. I wouldn't have it and asked them to give me 5 minutes and wait in the shop but not to open the door if some late customers wanted to browse around.

There were only a few things to collect, besides my toothbrush and a shaver and we were on our way. "Zinco, aren't you living in Bayswater any more?" Barbara inquired. "No. I sold my flat mainly because of the loss of my beloved Duke and the memories sometimes give me sleepless nights." "Who is Duke?" Andrew asked. "Duke was Zinco's dog for over 12 years and he got run over in Hyde Park not so long ago and he was a beautiful dog, despite his dislike for me. Maybe you've forgotten that I told you about it."

I wasn't going to talk too much about my financial affairs and especially not in front of Andrew and the only reason for me accepting their invitation was to talk to Barbara and collect a few bits which had been left behind on my last visit. As we entered the house, the overwhelming smell of lovely herbs and spices hit my nostrils. During the dinner I was doing my best to try to find out as much as possible about Andrew. I always thought that I was good at judging other people's character through talking to them. It turned out in the end that I was failing miserably on a few occasions and the only thing that I got right was: Andrew was a sly, slimy, smooth talking, cocky, young, spoilt brat! And I could see that he sensed that I was and could be a bit too clever for him. All that didn't bother me since my plans were different from his and if he thought that I was some kind of silly middle- aged man, he was mistaken. All that went through my mind later on as I drove him to St Albans train station after our dinner. At least he thanked me when I dropped him off.

Back at Barbara's place I noticed that all the dishes and the utensils were in a dishwasher and the dining room looked tidy. There was a new bottle of red wine on the table, next to the half bottle from which Barbara and Andrew had drunk. She looked at me, as if to say that there was nothing added to the bottle in front of me. I was actually glad that she had a big glass of wine. Up to that point I hadn't drunk a drop of alcohol despite Barbara urging me to drink some. I just wanted to be sober and listen to what she was going to say about her holiday and about her plans in general. I could see that the wine was already having an effect on her. She lost all her nervousness and was beginning to explain why she hadn't told me about her forthcoming trip to Ireland. I was listening and the more I listened the more I couldn't make sense of what she was saying. It must have been well after midnight, when she finally dropped a bombshell. "Zinco, I am pregnant!" My glass of wine nearly fell out of my hand. "What did you just say?" I asked. "Yes, I am pregnant, and you are going to be a father!" My head was beginning to spin so I filled my glass to the brim. I had a lot of questions and needed some answers. I suggested that she sat down next to me and tell me how far into her pregnancy she was, but she couldn't tell me the exact time frame. There I was with my supposed partner, who disappeared for over 2 months, without any trace and comes back to tell me that I am to be the father of her child!

"Zinco, I was hoping that you would be jumping for joy when you heard the news, but now I think that maybe you don't want to be a father." "Barbara, we have to talk a lot more about the situation. Why didn't you mention anything about your pregnancy in your son's presence and how do I know that the baby is mine?" "Oh Zinco, you are suspicious of everything I do. Please let's go to bed and talk about it all in the morning when we both have clearer heads." But I wasn't going to be distracted and told when to go to bed! I was determined not to allow her to groom me into some kind of feather duster. "Barbara, you go first and I'll join you shortly." I carried on sitting at the dining table and thinking of the situation which was obviously going to be life changing. I was thinking with lightning speed and put myself into different scenarios. One was: what would happen to her child in case her health deteriorated? The other scenario was: where would we live? And how would I adjust my lifestyle and my working pattern? And finally, what if the baby wasn't mine at all?

Then I heard Barbara's voice, again pleading with me to come to bed, so I finally joined her. She then kept asking me why I was in a sombre mood. "Barbara, your unexplained trip to Ireland and your pregnancy story is just too much to take in on the spur of the moment and I need time to think this through. For starters, why didn't you tell me about your planned trip which lasted over two months and you haven't contacted me once?" "Zinco, we don't live together and therefore I have no obligation to tell you what I am planning to do. You also don't tell me what your plans are and haven't told me about the sale of your swanky decorated flat either. I found out and that was the reason I did not tell you about my trip." "How did you find out that I was selling it?" She paused and said that she found my estate agent's offer letter about three weeks before she left, and the letter was freely to be seen on the back seat of the car. I had to believe this, since there were various forms and documents left on my back seat but only when I didn't have any passenger and mainly at the end of the working day.

With that Barbara's phone rang and it was Andrew. She spoke

a few words and then handed it over to me. Andrew sounded apologetic about the mistake he made. Apparently, he mistook my wallet for his! I at that moment was speechless. I remembered that I took my wallet out during the dinner to show him a photo of Duke. "Zinco, don't worry, it's safe and I haven't even looked at what's in it." "Andrew, I need my wallet because all my credit cards, debit cards, BBC petrol card and the driving licence are in it!" I just wanted to make sure that he was still on the line and said: "Hello Andrew, are you there?" He sounded a bit nervous and confirmed he was, so I tried to speak softly despite my built-up anger: "You'll have to take the first train and come back to St Albans with my wallet, because my BBC pass is in the wallet as well!" "Zinco, I can't come home because of my exams later on today and the only way out is for you to come up to Durham and collect it". I just couldn't handle it any longer and handed the handset back to Barbara and went out of the house and sat in my car fuming and told myself how stupid I was to ever start a relationship with Barbara. After a while Barbara appeared at the front of the house and walked across the road towards the car. I was too late to lock the doors as she placed herself in the front seat and asked why I had hurried out of the house. Before I managed to even open my mouth, she came up with a solution. She would pay for the petrol and a day's work that I would lose while driving to Durham to collect my wallet. Durham was a long drive and I wasn't in any state to undertake the drive. Besides, I had drunk too much wine and was well over the limit. "Barbara, I appreciate your offer and Andrew's apology, but my roadside assistance card is in the wallet as well. Would you ring and ask him to give you the membership number and also tell him the time of my arrival later this afternoon." I just couldn't be bothered to say: 'please'. I was exhausted and asked her to sleep in her son's bedroom and to not wake me up at all.

She just looked at me with her pouted lips and quietly left for Andrew's bedroom. It was some 9 hours later when I woke up and went for a shower. I could smell the grilled bacon and was in a better mood, knowing that at last, I felt well rested. Barbara was preparing a really good, old fashioned English breakfast with all the trimmings, such as black pudding, liver and mushrooms. She was looking for my approval of an array of different fresh rolls and French baguette, in short, she knew how to please a man when she wanted to. She had obviously gone to buy all the ingredients while I was still in bed. We, for a change, didn't mention what had happened earlier on and scoffed all the food laid in front of us with delight. She then led me back to her bedroom and opened one of the wardrobes and took out all the stuff she had bought for me a while ago and wanted me to put it on. Every single bit fitted me perfectly.

She then asked if we could take Andrew's telly and a few other bits to Durham at the same time. I asked: "What do you mean we?" "I have cancelled my appointment and will accompany you all the way to Durham and back." I suddenly realised that it actually wasn't a bad idea after all. Up to then we had hardly spoken at any length about her past life and plans, and come to think of it, it was mainly chit-chat. She was always very dismissive when asked about her mysterious incoming phone calls.

Above all, I wanted to hear her thoughts about her medical condition in general and welcomed her on board. The journey would take at least 4 hours and I had all the questions ready stored somewhere at the back of my head so to speak. She sounded very chirpy and began to talk almost straight away.

The things she told me were shocking but at least I was pleased that she revealed her many little secrets and am sure that some of the things she said were said subconsciously! She had a myriad of problems within her family. For example, there was an incident with her brother about 10 years before. She then proceeded to tell me what had happened in detail: " One morning my brother John came to my room and showed me a 'girlie' magazine and asked if my boobs were the same size as the ones in the magazine. I told him to go away but he just wouldn't go. He then got hold of my arms and wrestled me onto my bed. He was pulling down my panties and I was shocked at the size of his genitals. I told him to stop, but he didn't!"

What shook me were her words afterwards. "John kept saying that red haired women are always 'randy' and I was just the right one for him. At the time I got aroused and despite what was going on, imagined that some unknown man was raping me instead of him!"

The more she talked the more she revealed about herself and I was reeling at what she had told me so far and what more was she going to share? Why did she say that she would rather be raped by somebody else, possibly a total stranger? Finally, I asked her about imagining that someone else was forcibly having sex with her, she just vehemently denied ever having said that and obviously realised that I was digesting everything that she said. By then my head was spinning, but I wasn't angry. I was merely surprised how calm I felt after hearing it all.

We were some 130 miles out of London and Barbara wanted us to have a short break. We stopped at the next service station and had a snack and coffee. I began to see a very different Barbara. She continued to talk throughout the time we spent at the Burger King restaurant. She confirmed again, how bitchy some of her co-workers were towards her, how jealous they were because they knew that she was able to send her son as a single mother to uni and still manage to pay her mortgage. I was also slightly surprised at this, but dismissed any thought of her wrong doing, because her working 6-7 days a week made it possible to achieve the results she had had so far. We were on the road again and she again did all the talking.

I suspected her of being on a drug high and that she must have taken something before our departure, but there was no smell of any weed in the car. She also had a constant supply of various painkillers and strong nerve calming pills and prescribed anti-depressants which I saw in her bedroom and maybe her prescribed medication took its toll on her. And thus, the reason for her loose talk. I had to say something and managed to compliment her on the frankness and boldness that she displayed when talking so far. I wasn't even upset any more about unwillingly making this trip because at last I would have a better picture of her, what kind of life she had and her plans for her future. She quickly exclaimed that she had no drugs on her whatsoever and maybe sensed that she had to reassure me on this issue. She was under no illusion that, had I smelt any 'substance or substances, I would have stopped on the hard shoulder and asked her to throw them out of the window! I got the right answer and waited for her to continue with her life story. After reiterating what I had said to her a few times before, I wasn't trying to preach to her about my honesty.

The reason was simply because of my brutal selfish reason not to break the law, knowing the consequences, I always wanted her to be aware of my stance on morality. I even suggested that the medical opiates in one form or another should suffice to calm her pains and nerves. "Barbara, you don't need to drug yourself with any additional drugs which could be your downfall!"

"Zinco, I haven't taken any illegal drugs for the past two weeks." "Barbara this is a good start and please keep off them and quit them all." Throughout my lifetime, I have seen and witnessed all sorts of misuse of drugs: cocaine, meth, crack cocaine, glue and paint sniffing etc. I had always managed to leave the group of people, where there were drug users and gently melt away into the crowd or had left the premises altogether. She continued to talk about her parents, how they struggled to manage to get onto the housing list and were later on able to purchase the house where they all lived. She had a sister who was tragically killed whilst riding a motor bike and missed her badly and according to her, there wasn't a day when she hadn't thought about her. "One day my mum and I had a heated argument and she said that she wished that I had been killed on that day instead of my sister!"

Barbara expected that I would say something like: "that is a horrible thing to say" but I was told many times during my turbulent childhood by my father, how I should go and disappear forever and die. I was used to horrible words that were also very often spoken by my sister during every small argument. Therefore I kept silent and waited for the next salvo of her many revelations.

Her story of her move to Corfu was another, according to her, very sad chapter. Finally, she explained the real reason why she left her husband behind in Corfu. Apparently, while there, she had learned how to water-ski and was becoming very popular amongst the water-skiing crowd. Things got very heated when her husband's cousin began to make advances to her. He was constantly round their house and one thing led to another. Due to her husband's excessive absence the inevitable happened and they ended up in bed. "Barbara, how could you allow such a thing to happen and no matter where in the world you have lived, except maybe amongst Eskimos. It was an unforgivable act of betrayal in your husband's eyes and to his entire family." "Yes, you are right, Zinco and I know that now, and still regret it, but it can't be undone."

I paused for a while and quickly glimpsed at her and thought: How many more skeletons are there in her closet? I promised myself that in no circumstances was I going to make any judgement, at least not straight away, whatever Barbara was going to come up with during the rest of the day. I also had to be honest to myself about my past relationships. I was always looking where the grass may be greener and wanted to do more in my life.

The results were evident in 'the stock taking' of my life. Two marriages, engagements and many broken relationships left in the wake of my quest for happiness. But there was never any cheating on my partner whilst in a relationship. We were about 3 hours on the road and there had not been a single word spoken about her pregnancy! That was all that I was waiting for, but she continued to talk non-stop about other things such as her investment plot in Ireland which she got for almost nothing from her aunt. She engaged an architect who had designed a house with a view of the sea. She also had a wish to retire somewhere on the Mediterranean coast which had the right climate for her disease. At the end of her excessive talking I asked myself how she was going to achieve all that. The inheritance, which was due from her father's share in the farm back in Ireland, according to her, wouldn't be enough.

My mobile was ringing, and I answered it and it was John the controller, who wanted my help urgently. There was a lady passenger who was due to land shortly at Manchester airport and had to travel to Durham, not only to Durham, but to the same university where Andrew was studying! I really thought it was spooky and asked: "John, are you joking or are you serious?" "No, Zinco, I am dead serious." I just couldn't believe the coincidence and Barbara just sat there, listened to, what kind of job my controller had just offered and gave a thumb's up. I felt as if the hair at the back of my was standing up. Without any hesitation I accepted the offer and began to calculate the time I had left to reach Manchester after collecting my wallet at Andrew's flat in Durham. Barbara wanted to know if she should take a train back to St Albans or wait for me to come back for her to Durham. "You can wait at Andrew's place and I'll pick you up sometime late this afternoon and take you home." Since she wasn't a fare paying passenger, I didn't have to adhere to the strict maximum 8 hours of continuous driving and was sure that I would still have the strength and stamina to finish the over 700 miles drive in one piece. The trip went without a glitch and by 9 o'clock I was back to pick up Barbara to take her home.

She sounded tired but was again very talkative. "Zinco, it would be a very good idea if you invest some of your money in this project, which in a couple of years would double in value. I'll pay for the trip for us two to go to Ireland and you'll be able to see for yourself if the proposition is viable." This sudden proposition came out of 'nowhere' and I dismissed it right away as a no, no. She kept on and on about another investment on the Croatian coast which she had seen on one of the websites. Apparently, there was a place in Croatia called Trogir, which supposedly has some kind of healing effects on MS sufferers due to the soil and drinking tap water. The second proposition didn't sound bad and the asking price for the house right next to the sea was £37,000, which included a mooring spot for a small boat. The potential was there, especially when considering letting two of the rooms during the summer season. I knew the town from my tour guiding times in Dubrovnik when, a few times, I had managed the tour of the whole of the then Yugoslavia. I used to call it a 'mini Dubrovnik' with its high imposing walls that surrounded the medieval town. She went on reading the description of the property and I couldn't help but ask her if she had all this planned well ahead. "Yes, I did, and I hope we'll go to Croatia very soon and see if the house, as advertised is still on the market. I know you speak the Croatian language perfectly because you once worked as a tour guide there." "We can go half on the purchase and your cousins in Slovenia could do the restoration and would probably be pleased to earn some extra money and at the same time have their holiday as well." I must admit that it sounded very interesting and promised to look into it. What she didn't know, was the laws regarding a foreign national buying a property in Croatia. I knew someone in Slovenia who had a property in Croatia who a while ago explained the only way to do any investment in that country, was to form a Croatian company and have it properly registered at their Company House, in short not dissimilar to a UK law governing companies' regulations and laws.

At this point I wasn't going to go through hypothetical questions and situations with Barbara, since she had no knowledge of that country whatsoever and suggested that we should wait till we get back to St Albans and explore the possibilities and limitations through the Croatian Consulate in London.

What Barbara didn't know, was that I was waiting for her to say at least something about her supposed pregnancy. I WASN'T going to go into any partnership with her until I found out why we weren't talking all this time about supposedly our baby! Surely, being expectant doesn't happen every day and should be the focus of every day conversation. She finally went quiet and fell asleep. I knew from my years of driving experience that the worst thing for the driver on a long- haul journey lasting for hours is, when a passenger or passengers fall asleep especially when sat in the front seat. It is contagious and makes the driver sleepy. At about midnight we finally managed to reach Barbara's house. As Barbara got out of the car, I noticed a wet spot on the back of her short skirt and a wet blotch on the front seat, where she had been sitting a moment ago.

I wiped it off as much as I could with a cloth and said nothing. We didn't bother to eat anything, except I poured myself a glass of wine. Barbara asked me to book a car, which meant my car, to take her to Stoke Mandeville Hospital where she was supposed to have a check up. I booked it for 11am, just enough time to see her neurologist at 12.30pm and take her from there to work. Again, she went to sleep in her son's bedroom, just to give me a chance to fully recover from my driving marathon lasting some 16 hours. At about 11am we were on the road again towards Stoke Mandeville Hospital after having had a good breakfast. I was in a good mood, so was Barbara and again Barbara did all the talking. Again, I expected her to mention something about her pregnancy and again she said nothing. Whilst sitting in my car, waiting for her to emerge from the main entrance, I had a closer look at the spot where there was a blotch on the front seat of the previous night. It was still slightly visible and I was sure it had come from Barbara but left it at that. It was much later on that I found out the history behind it.

She finally appeared and it was visible that she must have been crying. I asked if she was OK to go to work if she felt so upset about some possible bad news in relation to her MS and she agreed. I rang my office and cancelled the journey from Stoke Mandeville Hospital to the BBC and at the same time asked them to also cancel my work for the rest of the day. One of the controllers went frantic since he had a few jobs lined up for me and needed me to urgently help him out, but he finally understood my reasons. I took Barbara home and she didn't say a lot on our way back. She simply just shut off and all she wanted was to go to bed. I obviously assumed that it must have been very bad news and gave her time to digest what her neurologist must have revealed.

I went to bed as well. Late that afternoon Barbara woke up and came out of Andrew's room to her bedroom where I was sleeping and gently woke me up. She sat herself on the bed and explained the reason for her crying most of the time during the drive back home. The blood tests were positive, which meant her immune system was failing her. She would have to inject some of the medicine herself on a daily basis. I consoled her as much as I could and felt really sorry for her.

Again, she mentioned nothing about her pregnancy but I chose not to pursue the subject, although by now, was exasperated and anxious to know the reason. She composed herself and wanted to know how much she owed for the trip to Durham. "Dear Barbara, I had a job from London to Manchester and back to Durham paid by the BBC and therefore you owe me nothing, but if you insist, then take me out tonight for a slap up dinner. She produced a wad of banknotes and insisted that I take it but I refused. Once back indoors she went to log on to the Croatian estate agency which had advertised that particular house which was in need of improvements.

I immediately recognised the actual section of the road where the house was. It was about 1/4 mile from the entrance to the main gate of the fortified and walled Trogir old town. The house was virtually some 20 yards from the actual sea, but it looked quite dilapidated. My cousins from Slovenia were no structural engineers, who would be needed and I estimated that the property was subject to a town and country preservation order. Barbara was oblivious to all the above and I told her about my conclusion in a simple way: "Even with all of your money and my own money there is no way that we would be able to bring this house back to its pre-existing state." Whilst discussing further, my mind was miles away. I had no interest in going into business with Barbara without finding out about her pregnancy and refusal to discuss the subject. She must have sensed that I had something else on my mind and wanted to know if I was prepared to enter the partnership with her.

"Barbara, you want to run before learning to walk. A while ago you left for Ireland in some kind of vanishing act, came back and told me that you were pregnant and that I am the father and hitherto haven't said a word about it. Now you are trying to coerce me in a nice and gentle way, to become your business partner!" She looked at me and calmly went to get her handbag, which I always thought was unusually large. She then rummaged through it and produced an envelope which resembled a formal hospital letter. "Zinco, please read this doctor's medical result report." It was a Stoke Mandeville hospital extended diagnostic report, running into many pages and after reading it briefly, despite all the findings written in Latin, I noticed two words: 'Utrumque Gravidade' meaning, the pregnancy at this stage was undetermined. I handed the letter back to her and told her about those two words. She then again went through her bag and showed a self-testing pregnancy kit, which, according to her, was positive. At that point I rested my case, took her in my arms and promised not to doubt her any more.

Dear reader, my life up to then only consisted of: work, eat and sleep, with extremely poor social life, if any at all.

9

Jill Dando's Assassination

"Zinco, you can move in with me and I'll look after you. You won't have any rent to pay and I can arrange with my building society for your name to be added to the title deeds. The mortgage would then be in both names and we will share the repayments forthwith. Would you like to do that?" I replied, "If it'll all be in writing, I would." And with that, I grabbed my glass of wine and drank it in one go. Her face lit up, took my hand and asked if 'I wanted some', the very same phrase she used on our second journey!

Despite being tired, we ended up in bed and she led the show all the way and I was smitten by her charms. On the next morning, whilst I was still in bed, Barbara came to the bedroom with a pile of papers and amongst them was a confirmation of our flights to Trogir in Croatia and the accommodation for the coming Saturday. To this day, I still can't fathom why I was willingly going along with her plans. It was the beginning of a catalogue of errors, which were sadly overlooked by me. The BBC operational manager, when I spoke to him, was a bit offish because although I was self- employed, he advised they were counting on me and would struggle if I took 10 days off. I took it as a compliment. After securing the shop, with a notice in the shop window to indicate the closure for 2 weeks, I took a lot of personal belongings and some other stuff and made my way to St Albans. At the time I believed that it was still not too late for me to finally have a family.

Barbara appeared to look happy to see me and even helped with bringing some of the lighter boxes into the house. She had already half packed her suitcase and even managed to prepare a light lunch. Barbara wanted to go to her bank and withdraw twenty thousand Euros, which would be needed to pay a deposit on the house in Croatia and I had a set withdrawal limit of £10k on my cash card.

My phones were ringing non-stop, but because I had notified both companies of my planned trip, I didn't answer them. Barbara was doing the last of her shopping and we went back to my new 'home'. Since I joined the BBC and found out how the studios worked, with all the techniques regarding the making of a TV series, I just couldn't concentrate on watching TV any more. I instead preferred to listen to the radio, if possible Classic FM, where there was a news broadcast during almost every interval, but on that day my radio was switched off. The shocking news was 'lurking just around the corner'.

After I had safely parked the car and had stepped into the hallway, the phone went off again and this time I answered it. It was BBC transport and John, the controller asked if I was watching the news. "Not yet." "Zinco, Jill Dando was shot a short while ago and we need you urgently. We are outsourcing our workload to other companies which is a shame, as this is costing us a lot of money." Barbara came running towards me and all she said was: "Jill Dando is dead!" As we sat down the 'news flash' was still on but with no clues and only a brief statement with the footage of the crime scene in Govan Avenue, Fulham. It was only 10 days since I last drove her and her fiancé Alan to Heathrow.

Immediately the name Vojo, the driver whom I introduced to my second company came to mind as a suspect. I rang 'Niven

Cars' and the whole company was already in shock. I mentioned my suspicion, but the manager dismissed it. Vojo had some weeks prior verbally insulted one of the female newscasters and was sacked on the spot. I am still to this day adamant and convinced that he had had at least something to do with Jill's assassination! Especially since he insisted that I introduce him to the BBC once I had brought him into Niven Cars. All sorts of images of him came to mind. His demeanour, his way of talking, the way he dressed and many other things, just made me think and ponder. His car was a top of the range Mercedes Benz but a left- hand drive. Maybe, just maybe, he was on some kind of a mission. Was the Serbian government sending him and his car to the UK to do some harm, since it happened at the height of Milosevic's power struggle? I was never able to find out, why nobody from Niven Cars had contacted the BBC directly after the driver Vojo was dismissed in my presence. Niven Cars should also have contacted the BBC security department and made them aware of Vojo's sacking and have his badge annulled.

The same newscaster was driven by me on the next morning and these were her words: "The driver from your company, Mr Vojo, shouted at me the other day and used obscene language and in his rage told me not to broadcast the bombing of Serbia and Belgrade again. He told me he is a proud Serb who has a family and that it was a criminal act of the Allied forces to bomb his country!" I still wonder if her complaint was taken seriously and if not immediately, at least after Jill's murder why I had not been briefed about the incident. Vojo was still in the possession of his badge which still gave him access to the BBC and was with impunity roaming through the whole BBC complex.

My statement about Jill Dando is as follows: I was NOT Jill Dando's 'ROCK'! I merely drove her on 10-12 occasions, for the reasons mentioned in one of the previous chapters. Miss Dando always paid for her journey in full at the end of her journey. Miss Dando was devoted to her partner Alan and I NEVER SPOKE about her private life or any other work she did. She always insisted she sit in the front passenger seat, for reasons mentioned in one of the previous chapters. I am not criticizing the UK police force on how they did or didn't do their work in handling her assassination. In the aftermath, I gave one of the CID officers my business card whilst waiting for my passenger in the BBC lobby, as he waited for his driver.

It was after the airing of 'Crime Watch UK'. At the time, I still remember mentioning my suspicion about Vojo, but haven't heard anything ever since. Was the person, whom I gave my card to, a CID officer at all? I presume the police's concentration was focused on the suspect, who was later on exonerated. Once, after a few years, I contacted one of the managers at the then Niven Cars Company and wanted to get some information about Vojo, the driver, but the company had been sold on and he was out of a job. Niven Sinclair himself died and I read shocking facts about his convictions and imprisonment, namely being a convicted paedophile! How he slipped through the BBC strict vetting process, is still a mystery. I just didn't know all that, because at the time had no reason to question his integrity. I SHOULD HAVE URGED THE NIVENS' PROPRIETOR TO SACK THE DRIVER, VOJO SOONER, SIMPLY BECAUSE OF HIS HATRED OF

THE UK. DESPITE THE FACT THAT I INTRODUCED HIM TO THE COMPANY. I SHOULD ALSO HAVE PURSUED THE INCIDENT WITH THE FEMALE NEWSCASTER WHO WAS VERBALLY ASSAULTED BY THE ABOVE MENTIONED DRIVER. MORE IMPORTANTLY, TO REPORT THE INCIDENT TO THE BBC AT THE HIGHEST POSSIBLE LEVEL. I HAD NO AUTHORITY TO GO ANY FURTHER WITH MY SUSPICIONS. AND FINALLY, THERE MUST BE THE BBC SECURITY CAMERA RECORDS STILL IN THEIR ARCHIVES WHICH WOULD SHOW THAT NIVEN'S DRIVER IMAGES, INCLUDING HIS CAR DETAILS.

My thoughts, at the time were wondering at the weird coincidence, that on that day, 26th April 1999, the day of Jill Dando's assassination, it was my 'name day'! I had a duty to the BBC, which always remunerated me handsomely, to without any hesitation call them and confirm that I was 'on board' and ready to work. The next thing was to tell Barbara to cancel the trip. She raised her voice and wanted to appear firm and with her pouted lips began to throw her 'toys out of the pram.' "It's easier said than done and I have spent a lot of money on this trip. We are going and that's it." I wasn't going to be swayed by her persistence and changed my clothes, put on a trademark bow tie and was ready to go. Her phone rang and she called me to wait for her, because her superior wanted her to come to work, also due to the high volume of work due to the sudden death of Jill Dando.

On our way to London Barbara didn't say a lot and that suited me. She went through the main entrance and I used the drive-in gates. The security was visibly stepped up and I was asked for the first time to open my boot. During that afternoon I made a dozen short trips to different studios with some foreign correspondents. At about 11pm I took a break and drove to a small, quiet car park about 1/2 mile from the BBC. The car park was situated next to Wormwood Scrubs Common. There was always enough space during the night and I parked my car at the far end. As I was unwrapping my KFC lunch box, Barbara called and asked if I was anywhere near the studios. Out of fear for and not wanting any possible argument I told her that I was somewhere in town but still asked when her shift ended and that I would take her home. I booked her car for 12.30am. I opened the window and began to munch my fried chicken. I listened to the radio and all stations were digesting the tragic incident. Another two cars parked next to me and both drivers stepped out of their cars and went for a stroll. The only lit area was at the entrance to the car park, but the rest was in darkness. My eyes caught a glimpse of a woman, wearing a white duvet coat, exactly the same as Barbara's. She walked along the bushes and suddenly disappeared between the trees. I found it very strange seeing a woman walking in the darkness alone. After a while, the same woman was walking back towards the exit and continued to walk along the main road towards Shepherd's Bush. Soon after Barbara rang again and asked the same question of my location and that she was ready to go home. I called one of my head controllers Phil and signed off. He expressed his appreciation for my help and was aware of the cancellation of my trip just to help them out. Barbara was already outside the main entrance and we were on our way. She looked tired but was still talking about how busy the whole afternoon had been. "I think that you were right to call off the trip, Zinco. I managed to postpone the trip for 2 weeks without any extortionate penalties."

"But Barbara you shouldn't have rebooked this trip for another date without consulting me first and I don't like it one bit!" She went quiet for the rest of the journey. As we arrived home, there was a brown package with only Barbara's name on it at the entrance to the house. She picked it up and went indoors. She unwrapped the small parcel and suddenly the stench of rotten fish hit me! I also noticed a bit of mud on the back of her coat and asked her if she had fallen and she said "yes, on the BBC stairs earlier on." "Zinco, I have had a parcel with dead fish inside it twice before, and I don't know why." "I'll tell you why, and it's only a guess. The mafia uses this method if someone has a grudge against another person. Have you upset someone in the past?" "Definitely not!" "Let's bin it" was my suggestion "and have some rest." She went to sleep in her son's room again, claiming that I snore. It was the first time in my life that I had heard that. It suited me anyway because I was too tired to discuss the subject any more.

The day of Jill Dando's funeral was again a very busy time. Again, I had no strength nor the authority to pursue my suspicion about the driver Vojo (the Serb) who, in my opinion, most probably killed her. I also took into account that the police already had a suspect in custody.

Barbara managed to cancel the second booking but at a cost. It took a while to convince Barbara that she shouldn't book anything that had any connection with my name again without asking me first. We were working all hours and I began to neglect the shop. I stopped going to the auctions to replenish the stock. Barbara wanted me to take her to a few places all the time and every time I asked about the baby, she produced many different scans.

After two months I agreed for us two to go by car to Croatia via Switzerland, and whilst in Switzerland, stay at one of the hotels where I worked many years ago. The property in Croatia was still on the market and we formed a proper certified limited company and put the deposit on that house in the name of the company. We jointly deposited forty thousand euros with the Croatian bank. The completion was due in four months. Strangely, the company is still listed on the Croatian website as Zdenko & Braid. We also visited my home- town in Slovenia and discussed with two of my cousins our plan to renovate the house. They were ready to go to Croatia at any time and start the work.

We returned safely and a few days afterwards, out of the blue, Barbara popped the question: "Are we getting married or not?" I thought that that was the most cold hearted marriage proposal I had ever heard someone ask a partner!

"Please give me more time, Barbara, because there are so many things to be sorted out before we are ready to get married and I promise, the moment the baby is born, I'll honour my promise. We also have to sort out my snoring problem, if that's the reason for you sleeping in your son's room." To this day the way she popped the question still echoes in my ears. I was again feeling sorry for her and tried to understand the reason for the way she said those words in such an unromantic manner.

My post, which was redirected to my new address, simply wasn't coming, although I had paid for my mail to be redirected. I checked with my bank and direct debits were being collected as usual. I at that time wasn't particularly alarmed, but the problem had to be addressed soon. I asked Barbara if there was a possibility of someone intercepting my mail and she assured me that to the best of her knowledge she never missed her mail. I went to my shop and checked if there was any mail but found only a pile of leaflets and junk mail. That night I stayed in the flat to open the shop the next day. I started at 2am on Sunday morning to take as much of the stuff as possible out of the shop.

Arnold gave me a couple of white wallpaper rolls and by 7am I was open for trade and used the wallpaper to write in big letters: CLOSING DOWN SALE! Most of the stall holders and Arnold were wondering why I was closing down and surprisingly, I had no answer. People sometimes do things on the spur of the moment and I was then doing just that. Barbara was calling throughout the night and morning, until I finally answered. She was on her way to the shop. There was sudden mayhem, with people trying to get their hands on the bargains. My two loyal helpers were busy bringing more stuff out of the basement. By the time Barbara came, most of the good stuff had sold including the rest of the chandelier bits. Yes, I did have a few thousand in my pocket, but what was more important, was the feeling that there wouldn't be any more memories of my lost pet Duke.

There won't be any more questions about how Duke died or if I am suing the woman who drove over poor Duke and so on. People who obviously adored him didn't understand that every time they asked me about Duke I felt a pain in my back as if someone was stabbing me. At about 2pm I went to collect my three boxes full of the most expensive items, which were sorted before the shop opening. There were some other bits which I gave to my two helpers who were visibly upset by the closure of the shop due to it being their small weekly income for a good while.

When we got home Barbara wasn't feeling well and she went to bed in Andrew's room. I wanted to find out if I was really snoring and went to find my digital recorder and placed it under my pillow. The recorder had the capacity of 50 hours of continuous recording. The next morning, I was anxious and went to the garden and tried to find the recorded snoring. There was no snoring recorded. I kept quiet about it. Barbara was calling from downstairs, to come and talk to my booking office. John the controller wanted to know if I wanted to go to Paris with a group of Italian reporters as repayment for my show of loyalty on the day of Jill Dando's death. He asked me to collect all the paperwork and the Channel Tunnel tickets. The job was in two days' time. "Hey John, I appreciate it a lot and I would do the favour again if needed without expecting any reward afterwards!" Barbara asked what the job entailed and I just said that it was a two day job, with an overnight stay in Sangatte in France, commencing in two days.

Barbara prepared a breakfast and we were on our way to work. I collected the paperwork for the job and John thanked me again for helping him out such a long time ago and produced another envelope with my name on it. It was from Klauss and inside were ten £50 notes and a note saying thank you and an apology for the cancellation of our tour. There was not much work and I needed some rest and time off anyway. The last month had been absolutely hectic and I wanted to be well rested for the upcoming trip to France. By then, most of the cash was paid into my account.

Barbara wanted to finish her work early and we were back home by 7pm, had our dinner and she went this time to our bedroom, and shut the door. I could hear her talking to someone and I presumed that it was Andrew.

At about 3am I went upstairs and she just lay there expressionless. When asked if something was wrong she just said that Andrew wasn't well and hastily retreated into his room. I, for the first time noticed that there were cracks around the door frame and I could hear her loud whispering coming through the cracks. The frame was actually supporting the adjoining plaster board wall of Andrew's room. I thought she was dreaming and was bemused, since it was her talking during her sleep, not my snoring that disturbed her sleep. I was wrong! She didn't go to work the next day and I went to see the landlord of the shop. He was surprised to see me and asked for the keys. I was equally surprised by that question and he noticed it.

Apparently he had been trying to contact me, but since he had no reply, he took repossession of the shop and the flat, due to non-payment of rent. He produced copies of some five recorded letters, all addressed to my new address in St Albans. I gave him the keys and said nothing and left. Although I closed the shop, it was my intention to keep the two flats. It was another blow to my self-esteem and the end of Brick Lane! I even forgot to ask him what had happened to some of the items left in the flat. When I got back, Barbara wasn't at home. She had left a note saying that she had changed her mind and that she would be at work and would call me in due course. That suited me, since I was sure there must be many of my letters sent to this address. Barbara had an old fashioned, but not antique chest under her bed which was locked.

10

The 'Other' Barbara

At least by then, I was certain that my letters were in there, locked away. I collected her as usual and didn't say a word about my shop being repossessed and equally didn't mention her locked chest, tucked under the bed. I planned to wait for the moment when Barbara was at work, and then simply drag the chest and most of my belongings out of the house and rent a room at one of the Bed and Breakfasts in the area. After she came home, we hardly spoke, and for a change she slept next to me, but I fell asleep very quickly.

Early next morning, I dressed in my 'Sunday best' and without saying goodbye to Barbara, left to pick-up my passengers from their hotel in London. Despite my doubts and suspicions about my missed mail and Barbara's pregnancy, I felt great. The passengers were a very jolly group of Italians and with a great sense of humour.

As we approached the Eurotunnel check point they began to look for their passports. One of them, Antonio, started to swear in Italian. They very quickly realised that their passports were still at the hotel reception. I was able to understand that they had also left their other personal identification papers in their bedroom safes. Antonio asked if we had an open type Eurotunnel ticket and would they have me as their driver again but at that time I didn't know. It was obvious that they were resigned to the fact that we had no choice but to turn around and head back to London. I walked to the check point and asked the officer to help us to turn around, since my passengers hadn't any valid travel document. The BBC was contacted and advised me to take them back to their hotel, collect their signatures on my daily sheet and I would be advised in due course.

My journey to Folkestone and back would be paid and the Eurotunnel tickets should be returned to our booking office forthwith. It was about 3pm by the time I finished the journey back to London and handed in my daily sheet and the Eurotunnel tickets. Barbara kept ringing, messaging and asking how the trip was so far, and when would she see me again. At that point I changed my mind about telling her what happened and wanted to surprise her with my early return to St Albans. In my mind I already had a plan of how to go about my moving out of the house without her suspecting anything.

On my way I stopped at Marks and Spencer and bought some ready meals, a single red rose and hit the M1 motorway. I got stuck in traffic because of an accident which had happened earlier and all three lanes were blocked. It took four hours before all the lanes were open again and by 11pm I arrived at my 'new home.' I parked the car and quietly walked towards the entrance. The dimmed lights were on and I gently turned the key in the lock and took my shoes off so as not to wake up Barbara.

Suddenly there were some noises akin to someone quite loudly moaning and whimpering in ecstatic enjoyment, coming from the ground floor living room, just a few feet away. Slowly, like a cat I walked towards a slightly opened door, and stopped. Barbara's words then hit me: "F**K me, Andrew, F**k me hard and give it to me." At that moment I felt as if my legs were made of lead, weighing a ton! My knees were getting wobbly but I still managed to take another step towards the ajar door.

There she was, bent down on all fours, naked, her back turned in my direction. Andrew was humping her from behind, totally immersed and oblivious to my presence! I froze. It took some time to take my eyes off what I had just seen. It took me more time to turn round, without any noise and collect my shoes, step outside and gently close the front door. At that moment, I just couldn't find where I had parked my car. A few houses further down the road I had to sit down on someone's front garden steps for a few moments and suddenly noticed that my car was right in front of me! I must have had a temporary memory lapse. I opened the door and looked for the packet of cigarettes which were for any of my passengers who might have forgotten theirs. With my hands trembling uncontrollably, I ripped the pack open and lit one of the cigarettes. Up to then, I hadn't been smoking and at the first inhalation, I coughed and felt dizzy and sick at the same time. My first reaction was to go back to the house and beat both of them to a pulp. I was back then still fast enough, vicious enough and ready to fight and defend myself and my existence. Deep down, at that moment, I knew that my future looked very, very bleak. I also anticipated that Barbara and Andrew would vehemently deny it all if I confronted them.

I began to shiver and sweat at the same time, and my brain went into overdrive and I felt that the instinct for survival cut in, just in time not to do anything stupid and make things worse. I then began to tell to myself, how silly it would be, to walk back to the house and start beating them up and how important it was to stay calm and opt for 'plan B'. But there wasn't any 'plan B' nor any other plan! And then I thought, if I go back at that moment, they would probably still be 'at it' and probably accuse me of violence of some sort, just to defend their 'innocence.' I was even thinking of calling the police, and have them arrested or at least questioned, but what good would that do me? The most important thing for me was to collect my belongings and that damn wooden chest with my lost correspondence and with God knows what else hidden from me in that chest!

I had an urge to get away from that house before, I might succumb to the temptation of going back and possibly causing real carnage in the house. I drove down the narrow lane towards the small wooded area. The tears were running down my face and I had to stop at the first available wide spot, so that cars could pass by. I couldn't properly see due to my tears and the burning sensation in my eyes. All I can remember were my screams and my howling like a wounded animal for some time. It took me a while to calm down. I lit another and then another cigarette, still madly coughing and by then, totally confused I tried to think clearly about what to do, but simply couldn't concentrate on anything. With a long day of driving behind me, I felt totally drained of my strength and fell asleep. It was the birds that woke me up and I realised, that in whatever state of emotion, I would have to go back to the house and pretend that I wasn't in the house 5 hours before. I knew that that would be a very hard act to pull off, but it would have to be done since I had nowhere to go, with the shop now gone.

Barbara must have heard my car outside the house and opened the door. She looked tired and exhausted. She didn't look into my eyes, but I could see the rings of tiredness around hers. Her hair was ruffled and it appeared that she wasn't expecting me at all. She briefly went on to say that Andrew had paid her an unexpected visit and that he would be leaving shortly. Andrew came downstairs, said hello, kissed Barbara on her cheeks and left, also looking tired! I, deep inside congratulated myself for handling the unbearable situation quite well and anticipated that I'd get even better with time at concealing my disgust towards them. The deep inner search for the reason why I had been chosen to witness the incest, began.

"Zinco, if you go to bed with Barbara, her son will probably join you too." These were the words, some three years ago, spoken by Shaun, the driver, mentioned in my earlier chapter! How ironic, that all of a sudden, these words literally came back to haunt me!

Barbara looked relieved that Andrew was out of the house and on his way back to Durham because the 'corpus delicti' wasn't present any more. She asked about my early return and if I wanted to have breakfast. To my surprise I said yes and went to the bathroom. I had a quick shave, had a shower and joined her at the table. Afterwards we went to the front room-lounge. I couldn't resist mentioning in a polite way, about how tired she looked and she was very speedy with her answer. "Ah Zinco, Andrew came late last night, and we were talking about his father and about many other things, as well as about the house in Croatia. The time passed very quickly, especially when we spoke about the plans with the plot of land in Ireland." I pretended to enjoy her explanation and egged her on to talk a bit more about Andrew and his plans and future. She eventually asked how my trip went and was I tired and had I wanted to go to bed. "Yes Barbara and you must be tired too, being up all night," but nearly blabbed out: "You have kept something else 'UP' all night too!"

And as I got up to go to bed, there was my little digital recorder under the two-seater sofa! I wondered how on earth the recorder had ended up under the sofa, whereas it should have been under my pillow upstairs! I frantically tried to distract Barbara's attention and asked if she wouldn't mind ringing my company from her cell phone to say that I wasn't feeling well and thus not able to work for a few days. While she went to fetch her mobile, I had a chance to retrieve my recorder successfully! Barbara ended the call and we both went to our separate bedrooms.

I wanted to find out why the recorder was downstairs. I could see that there were already 19 hours of recording on it. I tried to scan the digital audio files, and could hear nothing, and certainly not a sound of any snoring. I lay there staring at the ceiling and thinking of my next move. The immediate danger of me losing my temper and telling Barbara about what I saw nine hours earlier was over. Although angry about the situation I found myself in, I began to analyse what my greater anger was directed at. Was it their 'romping' which I saw, or was it the fear of the consequences which would inevitably follow? I came to the conclusion that since we weren't married and her lover was her son, and their secret, as shocking as it was, there was nothing to be done. But the thought of what my family and friends would say after she met them, if or when they found out about their, most probably since Andrew's childhood, regular 'sex sessions'? It dawned on me, that if they were doing this behind my back, what else were they planning, or had planned already!

The whole world caved in on me and the more I thought about it, the more worried I became. My primary concern was no longer the incest, since it was Barbara's body which they abused. I was glad to be able to separate the two huge problems and their conduct didn't really matter that much any more. My concern was about my investment in Croatia, my shared bank account with Barbara's, a pile of my other letters, such as possible unpaid parking fines, which were often wrongly registered against me, The Inland Revenue, insurance reminders, MOT reminders and at least a few dozen more.

At least for the time being I had a plan since there was only one issue left to be sorted out. There was no longer any wish to confront them about their unholy relationship and somehow I managed to doze off for a few hours. It was a bright day and Barbara sat in the garden and acted as if nothing, absolutely nothing in the world worried her. She greeted me enthusiastically as if we hadn't seen each other for a while and I found it very strange and she showed me a red rose, which she said was left on her door step by someone last night. Of course I must have dropped it whilst 'running away from the house.'

Was she assuming that I saw something during the night, and thus, she had a need to be nice to me? "Look Zinco, at this beautiful oleander plant, which you brought back from Slovenia last year and look how tall it has grown!" She told me that back in Corfu she had had lots of them, but not as beautiful as this one. "I still have the flowers which retained the lilac-white colour, despite being dried, somewhere in the house", she commented, while still admiring the plant, by then a small tree.

These words sounded odd to me and I asked myself, why had she kept and dried the blooms, whereby there would be many more this year. I watched her, the way she touched the tall plant, and noticed that she only touched the bark and the lower parts. I knew that she was aware of the poisonous flowering branches! In a flash my auntie's words came to mind, when she handed me that small oleander tree, warning me, never to touch the leaves and the blooms because they were very poisonous. She urged, that I wash my hands thoroughly after touching or handling the tree.

Despite my partial memory loss, I still remembered how sick I had been once before, after Barbara made my favourite Earl Grey tea which tasted horrible. Was Barbara already then trying to poison me? Was she capable of stooping so low? At that moment I told myself to be extremely cautious and not to eat or drink ANYTHING again in that evil house, not even a biscuit! My next move was to get hold of my stuff in that chest as soon as possible and temporarily store it somewhere in London. To add an extra worry, my sister rang from Slovenia and advised me that my father was dying. I went online and tried to book the flight, but despite several tries, none of my credit cards were accepted. There was no time to waste, since only one seat was still available on the next morning flight. I let Barbara know about my father's imminent death and asked for her credit card to be used to book the flight.

Once that was done, I logged on to my online bank account which showed that my account was blocked and their advice was to see the bank urgently. I wanted to drive to London immediately, but by the time of my arrival, the bank would be closed. Barbara acted alarmed and appeared concerned about my problems with the credit cards. Because of the little time I had left until my early morning flight, she offered me two of her credit cards that I could use whilst in Slovenia. I remembered how she on a few occasions used her son's credit card without being challenged.

There were so many things happening within the last thirty six hours that I began to panic but didn't want Barbara to see it. Firstly, the Paris tour cancelled, then the shocking scenes played out in the living room, my father dying and the problem with my credit cards! I only had enough strength to tell Barbara that I needed a rest and went upstairs and all but collapsed onto the bed. The dizziness overwhelmed me completely and I had presumably lost consciousness for a short while. She woke me up at about 8pm and asked if I wanted anything to eat or drink. I nearly said yes but began to realise what had happened a relatively short while ago and with the thought of oleander tree, I said that I wasn't hungry. She noticed that my speech was slurred and asked if everything was OK and I gathered all my strength to appear to be my old self again. In stuttering words, I managed to say that all I wanted was a strong drink. I knew, there was a whole unopened bottle of Glenfiddich scotch downstairs, and asked if she would mind bringing it up, unopened and with two glasses and some ice. I used an excuse for asking the bottle to be unopened, namely my wish to smell first that lovely scent. The flight was some nine hours away and since it was from Luton and I had decided that I was going to the airport by taxi, there was an opportunity, to at last have a good drink. Also to momentarily dispel in my mind all the problems that I was drowning in. She kept asking me why my lips were twitching whilst talking, to which I had no answer. What I in fact did notice was my sudden stutter and stammer coming from out of nowhere. I knew that not all was right with me, but to be honest, I didn't care.

I didn't care about anything at that moment, except an urge to get drunk!

I woke up and still felt tired, but managed to pretend to Barbara, that all was well with me. I kissed her good bye and left for the airport. There, whilst waiting to board, I had enough time to try to withdraw some cash with my debit card at an ATM. All I could get was £300 and at the same time the card was retained, despite my efforts to retrieve it. The Nationwide BS debit card allowed only £200 and was also retained, with a note on the little screen saying to see the card issuer urgently! I put it down to a possible security issue, airports being a hacker's favourite spot, and anticipated that once in Slovenia, any possible errors would by then be rectified.

It was late in the afternoon, when I arrived at my father's retirement home. My sister with her son and daughter were already there. Father had passed away some thirty minutes before my arrival and the doctor wanted to know, who was going to be in charge of his estate, regarding the signing of all the paperwork needed for the funeral.

I left it all to my sister, since she lived in Slovenia and already had the authority to oversee his correspondence and financial transactions, but without access to his pension bank account. The funeral was arranged surprisingly easily and quickly. My father's wish was to be cremated and within two days his urn was placed next to my mother's in our family grave. We had a small wake-reception and I couldn't wait to return back to UK, not knowing what to expect upon my return.

I had a dormant account in Austria and withdrew all the 3000,00 euros and closed the account. There were calls constantly coming in but I couldn't be bothered to answer any. Once back in Luton, a taxi took me back to St Albans. Barbara heard the door lock and came to greet me. She looked worried, and tired. At least she didn't ask any questions about the funeral and left me alone. I made my way to the bedroom and noticed that a lot of my things were missing. She came to the room soon afterwards and explained that with Andrew's help she had moved a lot of my stuff to the spacious new shed at the back of the garden. I was surprised by how she, in a matter of five days, had managed to have this huge shed built in such a short time. I was too tired to go to see if any of my belongings had been damaged when they were moved. My piano would definitely have to be tuned, and if left in that shed for a long period, the damp would make it unplayable.

My hands were by then shaking, but I had to keep calm and was buying time to think about this new situation. I looked at her and her face had a devilish look, almost as if she had bewitched me. Maybe she was expecting that I would lose my temper and possibly hit her for what she had done without letting me know. I would never do that, since this time around, I wasn't in any danger of being arrested because of the drugs belonging to her, found more than a few years ago in my flat in London. Back then I was ready to slap her face, but not this time, since it was only about material things and money. All I wanted at that moment was to go to bed.

I must have slept more than nine hours and woke up refreshed. Barbara heard the shower going and wanted to know if I was hungry. I was hungry, but just didn't want to eat anything, especially after what she had done and asked myself: "What is she going to put into my drink or food to get rid of me and what's the way out?" I then heard the back door opening and there was Andrew walking along the fence, his body partly covered by overhanging tree branches, towards the shed.

11

The Final Countdown

From that moment on, I lost any sense of fear and calmly walked downstairs and asked what was for dinner. Barbara cooked an Irish stew with garlic, onions and it smelt delicious. She filled my plate and the sliced crusty baguette. To me, it began to look like some crime scenes from movies, where a wife poisons her husband with a seemingly tasty meal! I wanted to go along with Barbara's play acting and asked where her plate was. And again the classic answer, just like in the movies: "Ah darling, I have had my dinner already!" I stood up and went to the kitchen and immediately noticed that the pot was empty and there was no sign of cooked stew for two people. She just looked at me, sheepishly and surely realised that 'the game was up.'

She suddenly closed her eyes and fell to the floor. I didn't want to touch her and called the ambulance. Then Andrew walked through the back door and gave me a look as if to say: "You, Zinco, will pay for this." I explained to the emergency medical team what and how it all happened and they took her and Andrew to the hospital. I expected the police to come at any moment and so they did. They mentioned her son's testimony that I had something to do with Barbara's fall. I asked the officer calmly, if her son Andrew smelt of weed and they confirmed he did.

The officer then asked if I smoked and if so, was it also the weed? When I said no, he didn't refer to the drugs any more. To them, it was normal smelling weed on students. The officer didn't at any stage interrogate me, instead he listened to the rest of the sequence of events and was impressed about my work at the BBC and they soon left saying that they would be in touch if needed. Since the other officer didn't say a word and appeared to be too old to be just a 'copper,' I knew that they had done some research on my background before coming to see me and spoke to me with respect. I wanted to tell them about Barbara's incestuous relationship and attempted poisoning, but changed my mind, since I had no proof.

Again, I would make matters even worse, because once the police were involved, Barbara and Andrew would most certainly falsely accuse me of threats of some sort and it would be me who would be forced to leave the house. Once out of the house, I knew, they both would have enough time to destroy any evidence which would tie them to the crime. They would probably in return accuse me of stealing their credit cards and the like. I was cursing the day I met Barbara and wished her dead! It was only a wish out of desperation.

I swore whilst walking up to the bedroom. Throughout the whole night I looked and searched for my letters, bank statements, anything that I could, to prove where my money had gone but found nothing. In the morning, I was one of the first customers waiting for my bank in London to open. The assistant manager was very sympathetic and felt sorry for me. He could clearly see that within a few months, the normal pattern of my banking had taken an unusual turn, almost spiralling out of control. I asked, why nobody had rung and warned me about all those irregularities, to which he hitherto had no answer. We made an appointment, this time with the manager.

I returned to St Albans and spent the best part of the day on the phone. The Nationwide Building Society wouldn't discuss my account over the phone, except for telling me that my account was overdrawn and closed. The same happened with the Royal Bank of Scotland. The American Express credit card account was also overdrawn by over £4K and they were already taking legal action to retrieve the monies owed.

I was at my wit's end and reckoned that the total debt stood at £15000 or maybe more at that precise moment, and there was nothing that could be done about it, at least not for the time being. I went to Andrew's room and searched through his wardrobe, under the mattress, under the carpet and found nothing. I didn't care if he saw me in his room rummaging through his stuff and was ready to have it out with him. Yes, I was prepared to beat him up there and force a confession from him. Immediately after thinking about beating Andrew up, I thank God, I came to my senses. My jury service experience taught me that I would be in the wrong and had no right to take the law in my hands and be his judge. My search continued and I came across some DVD's and a video tape.

The video tape looked very familiar and I recognised it as being the same as Barbara had in her bag so many months earlier, and I took it to watch it again later. I just couldn't sit still and went back to my bedroom and had another look under the bed and under the mattress. The wooden chest had gone. Right in the corner in between the bed frame and the mattress was my little recorder, which must have slipped from under the pillow and I continued to search through her wardrobe which was full of clothing and shoes. The next place to be searched was the shed and I discovered that half of the paintings, some silver tea caddies and part of my silver cutlery was missing as well. I was sure that a lot of other stuff probably wasn't there either. In all that confusion around me, I wasn't in a state to remember clearly what else was missing. I took my chaise longue and a duvet to the shed where I intended to sleep for a while. I went back to the living room and got the VHS going, and inserted the cassette. When I had viewed it such a long time ago, the part where Barbara was the 'actress' from M&S showing the women lingerie, ended with the text: "Hello boys".

THE FOLLOWING CHAPTER DESCRIBES GRAPHIC, EXPLICIT SCENES AND LANGUAGE. READERS' DISCRETION IS ADVISED.

I skipped the video forward and there was Barbara naked, being fondled and sucking two men's p*****s whilst being spread out on the lounge sofa. The remaining scenes were all about her being screwed in different positions with different men! On a few occasions during her romp she could be heard saying: "Give it, give it to me, fill me!" I just couldn't believe what I saw and was overcome with mixed emotions. I could clearly see that she wasn't faking her orgasms and obviously enjoyed every bit of it. It was a homemade video recorded in the very same living room where I sat, and all that screwing went on, on my lovely chaise longue!

Admittedly, at that moment, I was an emotional wreck and couldn't hold back my tears. I began to stammer to myself incoherently and couldn't figure out how to stop the video player or think clearly. My vision got worse and blurred when Andrew walked into the hallway and continued towards the kitchen. With my trembling fingers, I finally managed to switch off the video player and called Andrew to come into the living room and softly asked how his mum was doing.

I could see that he was taken aback by my calmness and gave me some bad news about Barbara's condition. According to him, the hospital neurologists had found a tumour on her brain and she would be kept in hospital for a while.

I wanted Andrew to feel easy and decided to keep quiet about the missing money, the VHS tape, about my witnessing of his 'romping' with his mum and about my missing belongings. He hadn't a clue about my plans and I needed to make him relax and give him time to feel safe, because otherwise he could call the police and as mentioned I would most certainly be the one having to leave the house, being accused of domestic violence. He even said sorry about his statement to the police about my involvement in Barbara's collapse. He then went to his room and after collecting his holdall said 'bye' and left for Durham and I made my way to Watford Hospital. Barbara was again in the ICU and was surprised to see me. I, at the time, didn't feel any sympathy for her and all I wanted was to talk to her about her reason or reasons for plundering my bank account, about my credit card's misuse and about my correspondence letters with all the bank statements. The pregnancy, the video recordings scenes would be served to her later or at least so I thought.

I had to be careful not to go too hard on her with the question about the money, and when she heard the word 'bank,' she turned her head away and said that she couldn't remember anything about money. There was no point in pursuing my questions any further and I had to leave it for another time. She asked me how I was and was I eating well and had I worked hard in the last few days. She went on to say, how she could only see half of the things she looked at. One of the nurses came by and asked Barbara how her sight was and moved her hand from left to right. Barbara could only really see, half the nurse's arm. I stayed for another fifteen minutes and Barbara just lay there and stared at me. She obviously was in a bad state and I went to see the same nurse and asked about Barbara's diagnosis. She confirmed the tumorous growth and that Barbara might be operated on soon, but that there was a chance for the tumours to shrink through powerful drugs. I went back to St Albans and went to an off- licence shop and stocked up with a few bottles of wine and spirits. I wanted to use my phone to tell the controllers about my misfortune and my current inability to work. They understood and gave me time to recuperate. When I dialled another number the voice message told me that the line was disconnected. My line was on a monthly contract and most probably the direct debits hadn't been paid and in the blink of an eye, I had no phone line.

I poured a big tumbler glass of whisky and gulped it down in one go, losing all the willpower that I used to have. The self esteem had all but gone and I was at a loss to be able to make any plans but knew I had to keep going regardless. I began, although already slightly intoxicated, to think of any possible reasons why Barbara and Andrew had done this to me. The thought of Andrew came back to my mind and it dawned on me, that Andrew, a good while ago, by 'mistake' took my wallet to Durham. He had then most certainly copied all my credit and debit cards and presumably on the orders of his mum, Barbara. She and Andrew were obviously able to use those cards at ATM's and spend my money online. I continued to try to think of any reason as to why was I treated so abhorrently by those two individuals and couldn't think of a single one.

I treated Barbara, despite her lies, with respect. Throughout some four years out of nine of knowing her, I drove her on many, many occasions to see her father some ten miles away. I took her many times to the train station, when she was doing night shift overtime. I did most of the cleaning around the house, repaired the roof, gutters, cut the grass and countless other chores, most of the time, paid for our dinners out and dinners in. I paid for many other things and THIS WAS HER REWARD.

The alcohol intake took its toll and I drifted off to sleep. Waking up was the hardest bit, since the reality sank in again and with that, I had a need for another drink. I lost the sense of time for over two days and decided to go to town and bought a pay as you go sim card and cancelled my monthly payment contract, just to keep the same number. I also needed small batteries for the digital recorder because I wanted to find out, why the recorder was found in the lounge. Even while I taped myself to prove it to Barbara that there was no snoring recorded, the recorder wasn't hidden or placed somewhere inconspicuously, but under or next to the pillow.

All I ate were precooked meals from Marks & Spencer. There was also a deep freezer, probably paid for with my money, packed with food to feed an army. Once back indoors I changed the batteries and began to scan the files. There were some thirty six hours of recording and I sped forward every two to five minutes and listened for any snoring, either by me or Barbara, since when I left for Slovenia, she slept in our room. The recorder had a voice activating feature and would only record when someone spoke or if there were any other noises. I kept pressing the fast forward button till the ninth hour. Its red light flashed whenever there was a the slightest noise. I listened and again could hear nothing. I put my earphones on and increased the volume and there was a loud whisper. It was Barbara's. I could at the same time clearly hear a buzzing noise. I fast forwarded again and again till I could hear loud laughter.

12

Let The Recording Do The Talking

These are Barbara's own words - exact and unembellished.

I went back to the beginning and could hear Barbara saying to Andrew how stupid I was to leave this recorder every night under my pillow to record my snoring ha-ha, ha-ha. I stopped breathing and my heart was thumping like mad.

Then her voice was saying "what a w****r Zinco was to think and believe that I was pregnant ha-ha"! Then there was a silence for a few minutes, till Barbara's voice was heard again, urging Andrew to f**k her. I skipped to the next file, where she was warning Andrew to not underestimate me, because she had seen with her own eyes how I floored two guys in Croatia, who tried to snatch her bag. And another one, out of dozens of recordings, was about our joint bank account: "Zinco, being such an idiot, signed the document about our joint account without properly reading it through, ha-ha." Other comments were: "Don't worry about the credit cards, because I still have the piece of paper which he signed whilst we were in Switzerland, to authorize me to use one of his credit cards." And another confession: "I approached a guy at Kings Cross station and led him to a quiet spot and lifted my skirt with no knickers on and begged him to 'feel me over and over again." His p***s was huge. He finally went up my a*s! I'll meet him again tomorrow night and this time want him to last much longer!"

It took me a while to figure out how it was possible, for that little digital recorder's batteries to last that long over a period of time, but now, after so many years, I have finally solved the 'puzzle' and got the answer.

When I left for Slovenia, I must have inadvertently switched it to recording mode, whereby the red light goes off after a while, to preserve the battery's life. The batteries lasted for over 3 months, thanks to the shut down feature, if there were no voices or noises close by.

Subsequently Barbara's talking to Andrew and previous talking and whispering to herself and her past sexual escapades - these adventures triggered the recorder to record. Although the recorder had fallen in between the bed frame and the mattress it still picked up her whispering.

It confirmed to me, that nearly a year ago, she was that woman in her white duvet coat, whom I saw disappearing behind the trees! There was more than an hour of her whispering about how she looked forward to being screwed by a big 'rod' near Euston station.

Another segment covers her reliving an experience, when she approached two Romanian men in a little park in Shepherds Bush and used the same words as when she proposed to me three years ago. It was when I drove her home for the second time when she lifted her skirt and asked: "Do you want some?" The places she graphically described existed in real life, therefore it wasn't just in her dreams or her fantasising about it. And whilst her vibrator was buzzing and most probably, talking to herself whilst vigorously masturbating, she named a few of the places around London. The bed creaking noises confirmed that she couldn't have been sleeping for long periods of time. The book would have had four hundred pages, had I included all the conversation and comments.

It took more than two days to listen to most of them over and over again just to make sure of what was said. I simply had to listen to them. By the end I was at my lowest point. What surprised me at the time and until this day, is that I wasn't jealous, nor was I envious, whilst hearing all the torturous comments about me. If there was ever any love between us, that love died instantly when I heard the tapes.

She came home after a week and as she walked into the living room just said: "Zinco, I want you to leave now or I'll call the police." "Barbara what are you saying?", I asked. "Zinco, I know what I am saying!", and her voice grew louder. "If you don't go now, I really will call the police and have you arrested!"

I wasn't prepared for these words from her, especially after I had visited her daily and despite her awful and damning words about me on that voice recorder, I was up to then prepared to reason with her. I wanted to retrieve my belongings, my money, running into thousands of pounds, through negotiating and then leave her. I couldn't be more wrong! I thought that she must have received the medication which stabilised her condition and must have discharged herself out of hospital. This appeared to be the case. She added that she had discharged herself and that she was going to sell the house.

By then I had finally had enough and almost exploded. My raised voice was more of a shout: "You are a spiteful bitch Barbara and Andrew is not any better. You are two of the most despicable people I have ever met. You have both conspired to plunder my bank account. You have lied to me about your pregnancy. You lured me into your web of deceit and held me in your clutches. You have been screwing around right under my nose. I now know that when I used to drive you, unpaid, from your home to do a night shift you were not doing the night shift at all!"

"You have been 'dogging' amongst other despicable sexual acts. I cancelled my work on countless occasions just to take you to see your father, your brother and even went with you to Ireland to your cousin's wedding. You had invited me to go to that wedding, but you paid with my American Express credit card! When I left you for a while you went to see the landlord of the flat that I rented in Chiswick and told him a lie about how I wasn't going to pay the rent. I got a notice to quit and you my 'darling', cleverly persuaded me to come back to this evil house!" I still had the energy to continue, whilst at the same time I just wanted to cry, again out of anger: "And do you remember when we went to Andrew's university digs? You most probably had sex with him, hence the wet marks on the back of your skirt and the slimy blotch on the front seat which I cleaned off the next morning!" "You Barbara are a whore and by the way I saw your 'darling Andrew' screwing you on all fours and edging him to screw you harder"! "That red rose you found on your doorstep a few weeks ago was bought by me and I must have dropped it whilst leaving the house as a distraught and psychologically broken man!"

I paused and waited for her reaction and what she was going to say. She went for her mobile phone and I, at the same time, with the recorder in my hand, started to play back her recorded loud voice: F... me Andrew, F... It was the segment when she urged Andrew to screw her harder.

"What's that?" she asked, putting the phone on the table. "This, Barbara, is your own recording when you had incestuous wild sex with your son. At the time you both thought I was in France! Just to let you know, I came back to the house on that night and you were on all fours with your son screwing you from behind! What you two are doing will affect your son's life forever, bearing in mind you two must have been doing this since he was a child. It's known as grooming. Andrew is your own flesh and blood! I will recover from what I saw but it'll stay with me forever too!"

I had tears in my eyes but still wanted to her to acknowledge everything that had happened and continued: "What about your video tape where you screwed with God knows how many men at the same time in this living room and on my chaise longue, which is still smothered with semen?" I went on: "You most probably wanted to poison me with oleander's flowers but for that I have no proof."

I wanted to let her know, that I meant business and that the gloves were off. I calmly asked: "My darling, you were heard to say on this tape that I was a stupid, crazy w*****r, an idiot and a p***k amongst many other names!" I still wasn't finished with my outburst.

"But are you all of a sudden not calling the police? You daren't because despite your medical condition, you've realised that I have ample evidence and the whole plot and deceit would come to the fore, and this time it'll be you who'll be taken away and tried for incest!"

On hearing that she sat herself near me, all her blood drained from her face, and wanted to listen to some more, but I sensed that she was planning to snatch the recorder out of my hand and possibly smash it against the wall. I just gave her a smile and told her to think about it and made my way towards the front door. "Zinco, please wait!" she pleaded. "No Barbara, I am not going to wait. I am, for the time being not going to the police either. But I will return in a while, just to give you time to think about it all."

I went to the car and turned the key in the ignition, but it wouldn't start. There was very little I could do, other than check if the battery was ok, but had to call the AA and have it checked. The AA found that the starter motor was faulty and was prepared to take it to the nearest garage of my choice. Thankfully it still had a manufacturers' warranty, so it was taken to the Mercedes dealership in Watford six miles away. My car had developed multiple faults and it would cost about £3000 to fix it, to be precise.

All I had was 3000 Euros and £300 in cash. I still had Barbara's Visa card but didn't want to give her a chance to accuse me of 'misuse' or 'theft' of the card which clearly showed her name. I, at that stage, had become paranoid about doing anything remotely wrong, that could be used against me. After the garage repaired only the faults that would let me drive back to St Albans, there was only £700 left in my pocket. To go to the nearest B&B, the money left wouldn't last long. After checking the list of all the faults my car possessed, I didn't want to risk using it for any BBC work, knowing that the car was almost not roadworthy. The MOT was only valid for the next two months.

The on-street parking permit was still valid and I drove back and parked it right outside the house. Barbara was in her bedroom and soon came down to the kitchen and asked again, to hear what was recorded and I refused. I didn't have it on me any more anyway because I suspected that she was probably planning how to get hold of that recorder, so I left it in the car's fuse-box compartment. The car itself had so many hiding places, that it would take a mechanic to find it in all the little spaces and crevices.

"Barbara, you can't hear the recordings and that's final, and all we can talk about from now on is how both of you will pay me back all the money which you stole from me." I continued: "The chaise longue is already in the shed, the shed which had been, in all probability, paid for with my American Express card. I am moving into the shed until you can come up with some kind of a repayment plan. I'll sleep there and wait for my money for as long as it takes. "And now, I will also take all that's left of my belongings there. If you or Andrew attempt to go into the shed while I am not there there will be trouble for both of you, namely I'll go to the police and the whole thing will be brought into the open. At the same time, I'll put the charge on the house, just in case you two 'bastards' are successful in selling the house. I'll also wash myself in the public toilet, so that I won't have to face you too often. And finally, how will you repay me and how long will it take?" I was already prepared to see her performance, namely the tears, her possible pleading and denying as much as possible. I expected her to say that it was Andrew's idea, in short, Barbara lied to me in the past with tears in her eyes at the same time, so nothing would have surprised me.

I looked at her and waited for her excuses and felt great knowing that I was at last out of her clutches. I was thrilled that I finally had the strength to tell her everything that I had wanted to say in the past! It took her a while to come out with some words, which were meaningless, spoken softly and almost incoherently.

"Zinco, from now on I will leave you alone. I know what you are capable of if pushed to the limit. I also know from reading a few pages of your book manuscript, that you were ready to shoot those car jacker-thieves so many years ago, on the border of Libya and Tunisia." She went on: "Andrew went through your things a few days ago and found most of the pages of your manuscript and we both read it at the hospital. The thought of your vengeful nature and your non-existent threshold of fear or death gave me a real fright. For that reason alone, I wanted you out of the house."

"Yes Barbara, you should fear me but for different reasons. The car jackers, who took me hostage all those years ago at the Libyan border were drug dealers, armed and I wasn't! Yes, I wanted to get hold of one of their AK machine guns and had I succeeded, I would have killed them all. That does not mean that I am some kind of 'gung-ho' gangster. I had at that time expected to be killed at any moment and was of course prepared to die in due course while defending myself. Don't try to change the subject because I will do everything possible to recoup my money, but legally. I am at this moment contemplating sending your extended family in Ireland a copy of the audio tape." I still pressed on with my, by now, raging voice.

"The video tape has gone, which doesn't worry me, because there was nothing illegal about it. The morality in this case is in the eyes of the beholder, but what bothers me is your integrity. You were licking all those men's genitals and doing the rest, whereas you scolded me if I swore out loud on the rare occasion! It's ironic, isn't it? I am advising you to look for my letters, any bank statements, credit card statements and our agreement, which I signed, that indicates all the details of my payments towards the mortgage. I paid it into your bank, which must still have the pay in slips, which were paid in cash."

"How much money have you got at this moment, Zinco?"

By hearing her saying that, my heart pulse went sky high and I replied: "Thanks to you two bastards, a couple of hundred pounds to my name."

"I'll call Andrew to come home and we'll talk, as long as you aren't sending the copy of the tape to my family and my place of work."

"I am at liberty to do what I want with the tape, but firstly I need to go to Slovenia because my late Auntie Hanika's husband Joseph is gravely ill and is dying. I am leaving my belongings in the shed and you better make sure that none of my items are touched. Here is your credit card which you gave me a short while ago, which is probably also paid off with my money, and I want you to book a return flight to Slovenia. I will probably stay for a week and when I come back make sure you take some days off from work so that we can go to Croatia to retrieve my €20,000 and close the account." What I really planned was to lure Barbara to Croatia, go to the bank and collect my deposited €20,000 and her €20,000, which was possibly also my money anyway.

On the morning of the flight I took the recorder with me, just in case. My uncle had already died the night before my arrival and the funeral took place soon afterwards. The whole family were at the wake and knew that something was bothering me deeply, despite my laid back behaviour. I went to see a doctor and had the AIDS test performed. To my relief the result was negative.

I used the time left to go to the nearby Croatian town which had a branch of the same bank as in Trogir, some 300 miles away, to enquire about the deposited money left some time ago. The money was still there but it would need Barbara's presence to release the money. There were a lot of missed calls logged on my mobile but I couldn't be bothered to return any of them. Most of the calls were Barbara's.

Luckily the car started straight away upon my return to Luton airport, so I went straight back to St Albans. I avoided going to the front door and instead used the little alleyway which leads to the ungated back garden and entered the shed, the doors of which were slightly open.

There I found a sight which shocked me, causing me to nearly faint and with tears of anger I loudly asked my self, how much more I could take before physically confronting them both. My stuff was strewn all over the chaise longue and on the floor. All my expensive suits were cut to pieces, my shirts torn in half, most of my paperwork torn up and the rest of my few precious items missing. I was stunned and at the same time angry, but my inner intuition told me to stop and think about my next move. It just looked surreal and I remembered telling Barbara how my two ex-wives, after a heated argument cut up all my clothes! It was like history repeating itself. I removed the pieces of my prized expensive suits from the chaise longue and wanted to sit down on it but noticed that the fabric lining of the longue was cut off and removed completely. The springs were protruding through the cushioning material, so I put some of the cut-up clothing on the top. I had no strength to do anything else but to lie down. I had tears running down my cheeks and those were not tears of sorrow but of anger!

It took a while to take it all in and I finally picked up the rest of my paperwork from the floor and stuffed it into the suitcase and rushed towards my car, without even looking back. I knew that I had to leave the place in order to not succumb to thoughts of revenge and not to personally dispense justice. I went to stay at a nearby Bed and Breakfast where I looked for some kind of solace in having a drink to put it simply, just to get drunk again. I knew that I wouldn't have enough money to stay at the Bed and Breakfast longer than a week. I stayed for another two nights and only ventured out to get something to eat and drink.

It was on the last planned night of my stay, when I was completely sober and sitting on the bed, going through my suitcase to see what was left of my paperwork, when my phone rang. I didn't even bother to check who rang and stopped it ringing. It went off again and again, about six times when I began to think that it was unusual for somebody to be ringing my number so many times in a short succession. When it rang again I could see that it was Barbara's number so I answered it, but the voice at the other end wasn't hers. It was her GP who asked me to come to his surgery if at all possible. It was about 7pm which led me to feel suspicious about the lateness of the call. He said that Barbara was in a bad shape and needed me to take her home and help her to collect some of her belongings. I just didn't believe a word any more and

207

ended the call. The phone was ringing again and after I answered it I realised it was the same person, who had identified himself as Barbara's GP and in a few words explained that he was aware of the rift between Barbara and me and regardless, she needed my help, because he still had hospital details of her next of kin, which was me! I decided to drive by the surgery and see if the story was true. The doctor's surgery lights were still on and a man was standing outside and waved and pointed at the space where I could stop. He shook my hand and just said that Barbara needed my help to collect some of her belongings, because she could hardly see and that I was the only one who knew roughly where in the house things were. "What about her son"? I asked and he couldn't tell me, since his number was unobtainable. "Barbara needs to go to hospital. I have organised the ambulance to come to the house in about 1 hour from now and I hope it'll be enough time to help you gather her a few things." He then went inside to collect her and helped her get into my car.

Barbara didn't say a word during the short ride home. She could hardly walk. All I did was ask her what she needed to take with her. She acted hostile towards me, but I simply said that her GP contacted me because he couldn't get hold of Andrew, thus I was the only choice for support. I admit that in the light of all that had happened with my belongings, I felt no sympathy or empathy for her nor Andrew whatsoever. After about an hour there was no sign of an ambulance and the only sign was the arrival of Andrew.

I got up and left them both in the living room without a word and went towards the shed and then could see the flashing strobe lights of the ambulance illuminating the nearby conifer.

After a while I realised that I had no house keys to do another search. The next morning Andrew came to the shed with a policeman who asked what my name was and advised me to leave within the hour with the rest of my belongings. I told the policeman that it was my residence as well and showed him my driver's licence with the address on it, but he insisted that it was a domestic dispute and that Andrew, Barbara's son, felt threatened by me and that I should seek legal advice and find a solution through the courts. I just wanted to make sure of what I was hearing and asked the policeman what would happen if I didn't leave, and he said in no uncertain terms, he would arrest me.

I had no choice but to follow the advice given and was out in ten minutes, that's all it took and drove to the NCP car park and left the car there. The Citizens Advice Bureau was very helpful and sent me to St Albans District Council. At that point I was technically homeless, and they were extremely helpful and found temporary accommodation. Before offering me something more permanent, they had to establish, whether I had really told them the truth and the St Albans police station corroborated my explanation and the reason for not being able to enter the house, which was my home for over 5 years. I hadn't told the whole story about the incest to anyone, because I had planned to wait until Barbara was released from hospital and then go back to the house, provoke Barbara to call the police and only then would I tell my side of the story, including producing the audio tape recordings. Well, that was my plan, but I couldn't be more wrong, since she never came out of the hospital again. There I was, after all my hard work and leading a clean life, ending up with nothing to show for it. Luckily, I qualified for Pension Credit, and it took a whole month before there would be any money paid into my new Post Office account.

I locked myself in the room and spent the last of my money on tobacco and booze. I found my Freedom bus pass which I had never used, enabling me to travel to London's Brick Lane to see some people who owed me some money. Although it wasn't a lot of owed money, every little helped and came in dribs and drabs. I lost any sense of time and kept wandering around St Albans and London. I sold the car for £1,200 which is all I could get for it, after trying many car dealers to obtain the best price. All of the dealers appreciated the car was a late model Mercedes S class but nevertheless, it was almost a non-runner. Had I had enough money, I'd have had the car repaired and would be able to work again. I had nobody at that time to lend me some £10,000 needed to bring the car back to a road worthiness.

I went back to St Albans Citizens Advice Bureau and made an appointment with a solicitor about my rights to stop the possible sale of the house. The appointment date was arranged in about 3 weeks. I heard nothing from Barbara nor Andrew for nearly a month, when there was an SMS on my phone from Andrew, saying that I should not contact Barbara or him. I rang the number and spoke to Andrew in a nice manner, saying that I had definitely never contacted them since my departure more than a month ago. He gave me the number and it was from my other phone, probably used by the buyer of my car. I didn't even ask him about his mother's health and finished the conversation.

I knew that she must have been in Watford General Hospital and made my way to go and see her if she was in a state to talk about my situation. All that mattered at that time was: Why I was denied access to my home, which was partly paid for by me, being without a car, without my hard- earned money, an income, and a total emotional wreck! Nothing, but nothing else mattered at the time.

The nurse remembered me from my previous visits and led me to her ward. Barbara hardly recognised my face and after I said hello, she just kept looking at me without any expression. I didn't mind the way she reacted and without any further words, I melted into the crowds on the main corridor leading to the exit. Her two cousins from Ireland passed and just gave me a threatening look. I realised that Andrew must have contacted them and probably blamed me for the seriousness of his mother's clinical situation. Surprisingly, I was even thinking of turning around and telling them what went on between Barbara and Andrew, but I thought it would be futile, and pointless for the time being.

13

Barbara's Untimely Death

It was nearly a month afterwards, when one of Barbara's aunties from Ireland contacted me and gave me the news about Barbara's death and a funeral date, with her wish to see me at the funeral. I went but stayed about ten yards away from the rest of the mourners. After the last rite was said, I began to walk towards the exit. Carrol, Barbara's auntie, came up behind me and tapped me on my shoulder and urged me to join them at the wake. I feared, knowing my bluntness, that in all probability, I would tell Barbara's family and the rest of the mourners everything what went on between Barbara, Andrew and me. It would inevitably lead to a fight with Barbara's family and other mourners and therefore I politely declined her invitation and hitherto have never answered her calls. In a sense, I decided to spare her of having nightmares, just like me, after hearing my story and the truth, what really went on behind the closed doors of my then home.

The next day I went back to St Albans Citizens Advice Bureau and asked to see the solicitor with whom I had made an appointment and to hear what had happened with my appointment. I learned that the date was cancelled and was booked for the following week and with that, I went on foot to see the house, my former home.

I could see from afar some three estate agents' bill-boards erected in the front garden, one of which said: Sold. It was another blow to my self esteem and deep inside I felt 'crushed' again.

In the following weeks I tracked Andrew down with help from

some ITV employees. He was working in Libya as an ITV crew member at the height of Gadhafi's crisis. I was planning to wait for his return to the UK and settle the 'score' there and then. It was only the thought of my service as a juror on two occasions in London Crown Courts so many years prior, that saved me. Had I known how things would develop, and all the consequences and my turmoil regarding losing the right of abode I would, as already mentioned, have allowed myself to be arrested all those years ago and subsequently the whole case would have been wide-open, and the courts would decide, no doubt in my favour. I'm still to this day having nightmares every so often, but I always end up with the conclusion that it was me who had allowed myself to be duped into the relationship with those two people. I can't fathom why I didn't check my bank account balances, and how were those two individuals able to distract me from doing just that. I fell for Barbara's sweet words, laced with 'poison'. This book has been, metaphorically, in writing for the past 5 years, and all this time helped me to decide to publish this book. I shed many tears whilst reading the chapters over and over again, especially when reading the last chapter and what the tapes revealed of what was said about me. I tried hard to analyse where I went wrong and all leads were, in a boomerang fashion, coming back to me. My experience by working, till up to recently, as a volunteer in my local St Albans hospital, thankfully worked therapeutically, and had helped to restore my psychological self-esteem. The saying goes, that it's unethical to talk and write about deceased people because they can't defend themselves, but nevertheless I decided to defend myself as well, because despite a few years since have passed, it still hurts. Had Barbara and Andrew made a silly mistake, and 'mistakenly' used any of my credit or debit cards, or by mistake 'misplaced' some of my paintings, bank records, silver items and the rest, I would probably try to negotiate the return of those monies and artefacts. Yes, when I met Barbara, she had had a medical condition. But is it right that any person with an illness has a right to meticulously and over a lengthy period of time steal someone's property and plunder and hack someone's bank account?

My life kaleidoscope reminds me of the famous Frank Sinatra's song: 'My Way'. I also managed to do so many things, such as rearing homing pigeons, playing the accordion and piano, being a tour manager, working in many countries and learning to speak and write a few languages, doing various jobs, gaining a private pilot's licence, running my own shop, dabbling in property, getting married twice and engaged multiple times, having my own driving school, and much, much more. EVEN THE MISTAKES I MADE ALONG THE WAY, I DID THEM MY WAY. Regrets, I have a few, but too few to mention, except meeting that Serbian driver, or was he from Montenegro? He still, in my mind, had something to do with Jill Dando's demise, and this is the point, where I rest my case on this subject. Obviously, my biggest regret is ever meeting venomous, wanton Barbara.

I HAVE TO THIS DAY NOT AND WILL NEVER VISIT HER GRAVE.

My book may also be considered a warning to every mother, who contemplates to engaging in any sort of incestuous relationship with her child, that the stakes are very high and can destroy people. Be warned!

And now after all has been said and written, and tears subsided, I firmly believe and say, that our lives are predestined and that our life and everything around us is an illusion and a dream anyway!

THE END

AUTHOR AND PUBLISHER:
Zdenko Ornig
Tel: 07399 587 377 ornigz1@gmail.com